LEAVING SUFISM

HOW I WAS GUIDED TO MONOTHEISM AND THE STRAIGHT PATH

Shaykh Muhammad Jamil Zeno

ISBN: 978-1-7923-7825-6

First Edition: Rabī al-Thānī 1443 A.H. / November 2021 C.E.

Cover Design: Salafi Designs

Editing & Typesetting: Razan Gregory

Translator: Abū Aḥmed Ayyub ibn James Elkins

Publisher's Information:

Authentic Statements Publishing
P. O. Box 15536
Philadelphia, PA. 19131
215.382.3382
215.382.3782-Fax

Store:
5000 Locust Street (Side Entrance)
Philadelphia, Pa 19139

Website: www.authenticstatements.com
E-mail: info@authenticstatements.com

Transliteration Table

Consonants

ء	'	د	d	ض	ḍ	ك	k
ب	b	ذ	dh	ط	ṭ	ل	l
ت	t	ر	r	ظ	ẓ	م	m
ث	th	ز	z	ع	ʻ	ن	n
ج	j	س	s	غ	gh	ه	h
ح	ḥ	ش	sh	ف	f	و	w
خ	kh	ص	ṣ	ق	q	ي	y

Vowels

Short	◌َ	a	◌ِ	i	◌ُ	u
Long	ـَا	ā	ـِي	ī	ـُو	ū
Diphthongs	ـَي	ay	ـَو	aw		

Glyphs

ﷺ *Sallallāhu ʻalayhi wa sallam* (May Allāh's praise & salutations be upon him)

ʻAlayhis-salām (peace be upon him)

ﷻ *ʻAza wa jal* (Mighty and Majestic)

RadiyAllāhu ʻanhu (May Allāh be pleased with him)

RadiyAllāhu ʻanha (May Allāh be pleased with her)

RadiyAllāhu ʻanhum (May Allāh be pleased with them)

Rahimahullah (May Allāh have mercy upon him)

Table of Contents

Foreword

Verily, all praise and thanks are for Allāh, we praise Him, seek His aid, and seek His forgiveness, and we seek refuge with Allāh from the evil of our own selves and our evil actions. Whoever Allāh guides, none can misguide him, and whomsoever Allāh misguides, none can guide him except Him. I bear witness that there is no deity worthy of worship but Allāh, alone, with no partners, and I bear witness that Muḥammad (ﷺ) is His slave and Messenger.

As for that which follows, I received a letter from a Turkish student from the city of Konya. The letter reads, "To Muḥammad ibn Jamīl Zeno, the teacher at Dār al-Ḥadīth al-Khayriyyah in Makkah al-Mukarramah.

As-Salāmu 'Alaykum wa Raḥmatullāhi wa Barakātuh (May the peace, mercy, and blessings of Allāh be upon you.)

Our noble teacher, I am a student in the Faculty of Sharī'ah in Konya. I took your book, *The Islāmic Creed,* and translated it into the Turkish language; but I need to print your biography. Please send me this information at the following address. Thank you for now, and peace be upon those who follow the guidance."

(**Translator's note:** The greeting, in this form, is not permissible to be said to a Muslim. Rather, this is for the non-Muslim who does not follow the guidance. As for the greeting for the Muslim, it is with the wording "As- Salāmu 'Alaykum wa Raḥmatullāhi wa Barakātuh.")

Also, some of my brothers from the students of knowledge sought to write the story of my life, including the stages I went through from my youth until I reached close to 80 years old. They want to write about how I was guided to the authentic Islāmic creed, the creed of the pious predecessors that is founded upon evidence from the Noble Qur'ān and the authentic aḥadīth. This is a tremendous blessing that no one knows except the one who has tasted it. The Messenger of Allāh (ﷺ) spoke truthfully when he said, "He who is pleased with Allāh as his Lord, and Islām as his religion, and Muḥammad (ﷺ) as His Messenger has tasted the sweetness of faith." [Muslim]

Perhaps the reader will find in this story beneficial lessons and admonitions that will let him know truth from falsehood.

I ask Allāh (ﷻ) to benefit the Muslims by it and make it solely for His Noble Face.

Muḥammad ibn Jamīl Zeno

1/1/1415

Birth and Upbringing

I was born in Aleppo, Syria in the year 1925 AD. It is unfortunate that the Gregorian calendar is widespread even in the Islāmic countries, except for Saudi Arabia. They rely on the Hijri calendar, and it is obligatory because it is an Islāmic calendar and points to the migration by which Allāh gave Islām might. According to my passport, which agrees with 1344 AH, I am now about 70 years old. When I reached roughly ten years of age, I entered a private school and learned reading and writing.

I joined the school Dār al-Huffāḍ and stayed in it for five years. During my time there, I memorized the Qur'ān with tajwīd.

I entered a school in Aleppo that was called The Preparatory Sharī'ah Faculty. It is now the Sharī'ah Secondary School and is subordinate to the Ministry of Islāmic Endowments. It is a school that teaches modern and Islāmic sciences, where I studied tafsīr, Ḥanafī fiqh, grammar, morphology, history, ḥadīth, and its sciences, and other legislative sciences.

The modern sciences that I studied included physics, chemistry, math, French, and other sciences that the Muslims excelled in such as Algebra.

I remember that I studied the science of monotheism in a book called *The Humaydi Fortresses.* It focused on the oneness of the Lord (ﷻ) and affirmation that this world has a Creator and a Lord. Later, it became clear to me that many of the Muslims, writers, universities, and schools that teach legislative sciences fall into this error. This is because the polytheists that the Messenger of Allāh (ﷺ) fought used to admit that Allāh is their Creator. Allāh (ﷻ) said:

﴿ وَلَئِن سَأَلْتَهُم مَّنْ خَلَقَهُمْ لَيَقُولُنَّ اللَّهُ ۖ فَأَنَّىٰ يُؤْفَكُونَ ﴿٨٧﴾ ﴾

And if you were to ask them who created them, verily they would say "Allāh," so how are they turned away?

[Sūrah az-Zukhruf: 87]

Rather, even the devil, may the curse of Allāh (ﷻ) be upon him, would admit that Allāh was his Lord. Allāh (ﷻ) said, informing of his statement:

﴿ قَالَ رَبِّ بِمَا أَغْوَيْتَنِي لَأُزَيِّنَنَّ لَهُمْ فِي الْأَرْضِ ﴿٣٩﴾ ﴾

He said, "My Lord! Because You misled me, I shall indeed beautify the path of error for them in the earth."

[Sūrah al-Ḥijr: 39]

As for the Monotheism of Allāh (i.e., in worship), which is the foundation that the Muslim is saved by, I did not study it and used to know nothing about it. This is the condition of the rest of the schools and universities that do not teach it, and their students also know nothing about it.

Allāh (ﷻ) commanded all of the messengers to call to it. The Seal of the Messengers, Muḥammad (ﷺ), called his people to it but they refused and were arrogant, just as Allāh (ﷻ) had informed of them:

﴿ إِنَّهُمْ كَانُوا إِذَا قِيلَ لَهُمْ لَا إِلَٰهَ إِلَّا اللَّهُ يَسْتَكْبِرُونَ ﴿٣٥﴾ ﴾

Truly, when it was said to them, "There is no deity worthy of worship but Allāh" they would puff themselves up with pride (denying it).

[Sūrah aṣ-Ṣāffāt: 35]

The polytheist Arabs knew its meaning, and that it is not permissible for the one who says it to supplicate to other than Allāh (ﷻ). Some of the Muslims say it with their tongues, and then supplicate other than Allāh, thereby nullifying it.

As for the oneness of the Attributes of Allāh (ﷻ), the school used to do a figurative interpretation of the verses of the Attributes of Allāh, just as other schools in most of the Muslim lands do, unfortunately. I remember that a teacher used to explain the statement of Allāh (ﷻ):

﴿ الرَّحْمَٰنُ عَلَى الْعَرْشِ اسْتَوَىٰ ﴿٥﴾ ﴾

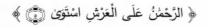

The Most Merciful istawā (rose over) the Throne.

[Sūrah Ṭaha: 5]

Istawā (rose over) means istawlā (conquer), and cited as evidence was the statement of a poet:

قَدْ اسْتَوَى بِشْرٌ عَلَى العِرَاقِ مِنْ غَيرِ سَيفٍ وَدَمٍ مهرَاق

"Bishr has conquered Iraq without a sword or spilling blood."

Ibn al-Jawzī said, "It is not known who said this poetry. Others say it was a Christian." The word istawā is explained in *Ṣaḥīḥ al-Bukhārī* with the statement of Allāh (ﷻ):

﴿ ثُمَّ اسْتَوَىٰ إِلَى السَّمَاءِ ﴿٢٩﴾ ﴾

Then He rose over to the heavens.

[Sūrah al-Baqarah: 29]

Mujahid and 'Abūl 'Āliyah said, "Istawā means to elevate and rise up."

[*Ṣaḥīḥ al-Bukhārī*, "Kitab at-Tawḥīd," vol., 8, pg. 175]

So, is it permissible for a Muslim to leave off the statement of the Tabi'īn in *Ṣaḥīḥ al-Bukhārī* and accept the poetry of an unknown person?

This corrupt interpretation that denies Allāh's elevation above His (ﷻ) Throne opposes the creed of Imām 'Abū Haneefah, Imām Mālik, and other than them. Imām 'Abū Haneefah, the one whose madhhab they teach, said, "Whoever says 'I do not know whether my Lord is above the heavens or on the earth' has disbelieved," because Allāh (ﷻ) says:

﴿ الرَّحْمَٰنُ عَلَى الْعَرْشِ اسْتَوَىٰ ﴿٥﴾ ﴾

The Most Merciful rose over the Throne

[Sūrah Ṭaha: 5]

"And His Throne is above the seven heavens."

[*Explanation of Al-Aqidah at-Tahāwiyah*, pg. 322]

I received the school degree in the year 1948, as well as the general high school diploma. I received a scholarship to Al-Azhar but did not go due to health reasons. In Aleppo, I entered the House of Teachers and worked as a teacher for about 29 years. Then, I left off teaching.

After I retired from teaching, I came to Makkah for 'Umrah in the year 1399 AH, where I met the noble Shaykh 'Abdul 'Azīz ibn Bāz. He knew that my beliefs are Salafī, so he appointed me as a teacher in Al-Masjid al-Ḥarām during the Ḥajj. When the Ḥajj season ended, he sent me to Jordan to call to Allāh (ﷻ). So I went, and I stayed in the city of Ar-Ramthā in the Mosque of Salah Ad-Deen. I was an imām, lecturer, and Qur'ān teacher. I used to visit the middle schools and call the students to the monotheistic creed, and they would accept it well.

In the month of Ramaḍān 1400 AH, I came to Makkah to do 'Umrah and stayed until after Ḥajj. I met a student from the students of Dār al-Ḥadīth al-Khayriyyah in Makkah. He wanted me to teach with them because they needed teachers, especially in the ḥadīth terminology. I called the principal and he made it apparent he was prepared. He sought from me a mandate from the Noble Shaykh 'Abdul 'Azīz ibn Bāz. So, he wrote to them seeking to appoint me as a teacher. I entered the school and taught the students tafsīr, the Noble Qur'ān, and other than that from the lessons that I would teach.

By the favor of Allāh (ﷻ), I began to publish small, concise, simple treatises. They were met with acceptance in every land in the world, and some of them have been translated to English, French, Bengali, Indonesian, Turkish, Urdu, and other than them. I named them *A Series of Islāmic Guidances*, and it has reached more than 20 treatises. Hundreds and thousands of them have been printed and most of them are free. The reader can find them on the back cover of the treatise with their names and numbers.

I ask Allāh to benefit the Muslims by it and make it solely for the Face of Allāh (ﷻ).

I Used to be a Naqshibandī

From a young age, I used to attend lessons and circles of dhikr in the mosques. A shaykh from the Naqshibandī order saw me, took me to a corner of the masjid, and began to give me the wird (their assigned portion of adhkār which they recite daily) of the Naqshibandī order. Due to my young age, I was not able to do what he commanded me with from the invocations. However, I would attend their sittings with my relatives in the Sufi lodges and listen to what they say in their poems and anashīd. When the mention of the name of their shaykh would come, they would shout with a high voice, and this surprising noise would disturb me at night and cause me fear and sickness. When I grew older, a relative of mine began to take me to the local mosque to attend what they call a khātm. We would sit in a circle and one of the shuyukh would pass out prayer beads and say, "Al-Fātiḥah ash-Sharīfah, al-'Ikhlās ash-Sharīf." So, we would read Sūrah Al-Fātiḥah and Sūrah 'Ikhlās the number of beads, while doing istighfār and sending salutations upon the Prophet (ﷺ) the way they would teach it. I remember from them:

"Oh Allāh! Send your blessings upon Muḥammad (ﷺ) the amount of creatures on the earth."

They would say it out loud at the end of their incantations; and after it, the shaykh who was appointed upon the khātm would say, "The noble link." They intended by that to imagine their shaykh while they are in a state of dhikr, because the shaykh connects them to Allāh (ﷻ) according to what they claim. So, they used to speak indistinctly and shout; and they would be seized with awe to the point that I saw one of them jump over the heads of those present from a very high place due to the severity of the state of his ecstasy as if he were an acrobat! So, I used to find these actions and shouting strange during the mention of the shaykh of the path. Once, I entered upon the house of a relative of mine, and heard a nashīd from a group from the Naqshibandī path say,

"Direct me, by Allāh, direct me to Shaykh An-Nasr, direct me. He who heals the sick and cures the insane."

I stood at the door of the house, and I did not enter. I said to the owner of the house, "Does the shaykh heal the sick and cure the insane?" He said, "Yes." I said to him, "The messenger 'Īsā ibn Maryam (ﷺ), who Allāh (ﷻ) gave the miracle of bringing the dead back to life, healing the blind, and healing the lepers says, "By the permission of Allāh." He said to me, "Our shaykh does it by the permission of Allāh!" I said to him, "And why do you all not say, 'by the permission of Allāh?!'"

With the knowledge that the one who heals is Allāh (ﷻ), alone, just as 'Ibrāhīm (ﷺ) said:

﴿ وَإِذَا مَرِضْتُ فَهُوَ يَشْفِينِ ﴿٨٠﴾ ﴾

And when I am ill, it is He who cures me.

[Sūrah ash-Shu'arā': 80]

Observations on the Naqshibandī Order

This path is distinguished by its secretive, hidden 'awrād; for they don't have dancing or clapping in them as opposed to the other famous Sufi orders.

This gathering upon dhikr, passing out prayer beads to everyone, the person appointed with the khātm who commands them to say such and such, and placing the prayer beads in a cup of water that they drink from and seek a cure from; all of this is from the innovation that the noble companion 'Abdullāh ibn Mas'ūd criticized when he entered the mosque and saw a group of people sitting in a circle with pebbles in their hands. One of them would say, "Say subhanAllāh such and such number of times" or do such and such the number of pebbles in their hands. He reprimanded them, saying, "What is this that I see you all do?" They replied, "Oh Abā 'Abd ar-Raḥman! They are but pebbles with which we count the number of times we say Allāhu Akbar, lā ilāha illa Allāh, and subhanAllāh!" He said, "Then count your evil deeds, for I guarantee you that none of your good deeds would be wasted. Woe be to you oh nation of Muḥammad (ﷺ)! How hasty you are to your destruction! The companions of your Prophet (ﷺ) are plentiful, and his clothing have not yet worn out, and his vessel has not broken yet. By The One in Whose Hand is my soul, you all are either on a religion more guided that the religion of Muḥammad (ﷺ), or you are opening up the door of misguidance!"

[Ḥasan, reported by ad-Dārimī and at-Tabarānī]

This affair is logically sound. Thus, they are either more guided than the Messenger (ﷺ) because they were granted success in an act of worship that the knowledge of the Messenger (ﷺ) didn't reach, or they are upon misguidance. The first assumption is absolutely omitted because no one is better than the Messenger of Allāh (ﷺ), so nothing remains except the other assumption (i.e., that they are upon misguidance).

The Noble Link is what they call imagining the image of the shaykh in front of them while they're making dhikr and looking at him watching them. Because of this, you see them in a state of awe, shouting with abominable, unclear voices. This is the level of 'iḥsān that came in the statement of the Messenger (ﷺ):

الإِحْسَانُ أَنْ تَعْبُدَ اللهَ كَأَنَّكَ تَرَاهُ فَإِن لَمْ تَكُنْ تَرَاهُ فَإِنَّهُ يَرَاكَ

"'Iḥsān is to worship Allāh as if you see Him, and if you cannot, then know that He can see you."

[Muslim]

In this ḥadīth, the Messenger (ﷺ) directs us to worship Allāh (ﷻ) as if we can see Him, and if we are not able (to worship Him as if we can see Him), then verily He can see us. This is the level of 'iḥsān that is for Allāh, alone. They have given it to their shaykh, and this is from the polytheism that Allāh (ﷻ) has prohibited with his statement:

﴿ وَاعْبُدُوا اللَّهَ وَلَا تُشْرِكُوا بِهِ شَيْئًا ﴿٣٦﴾ ﴾

Worship Allāh and do not join anyone with Him in worship.

[Sūrah an-Nisā': 36]

So, dhikr is an act of worship for Allāh (ﷻ). It is not permissible to join anyone in worship with Him, even if he is from the angels or messengers. The mashaykh are on a lower level than them, so it is even more impermissible to make them partners in worship! The reality is that imagining the shaykh while making remembrance is also found in the Shādhilī order, and other than it from the Sufi orders as will be mentioned.

This intense shouting that seizes them at the mention of the shaykh or seeking aid from other than Allāh (ﷻ)—such as Ahl al-Bayt (the relatives of the Messenger of Allāh [ﷺ]) and saints—is from the reprehensible actions. Rather, it is from polytheism, which is prohibited. Shouting at the mention of Allāh (ﷻ) is blameworthy because it is in contradiction to the statement of Allāh (ﷻ):

﴿ إِنَّمَا الْمُؤْمِنُونَ الَّذِينَ إِذَا ذُكِرَ اللَّهُ وَجِلَتْ قُلُوبُهُمْ ۝٢ ﴾

The believers are only those who, when Allāh is mentioned, their hearts tremble.

[Sūrah al-'Anfāl: 2]

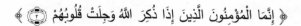

And in the statement of the Messenger (ﷺ):

يا أيها الناس اربعوا على أنفسكم، فإنكم لا تدعون أصم ولا غائبا، إنكم تدعون سميعا قريبا وهو معكم

Oh people! Be merciful to yourselves. For verily, you do not supplicate to one who is deaf or absent. Verily, you all supplicate to one who is All-Hearing, Near, and He is with you."

[Agreed upon by al-Bukhārī and Muslim]

Shouting, awe, and crying at the mention of saints is more severe in blameworthiness because this points to the rejoicing that Allāh (ﷻ) spoke of from the polytheists when He said:

﴿ وَإِذَا ذُكِرَ اللَّهُ وَحْدَهُ اشْمَأَزَّتْ قُلُوبُ الَّذِينَ لَا يُؤْمِنُونَ بِالْآخِرَةِ وَإِذَا ذُكِرَ الَّذِينَ مِن دُونِهِ إِذَا هُمْ يَسْتَبْشِرُونَ ﴿٤٥﴾ ﴾

And when Allāh is mentioned alone, the hearts of those who do not believe in the Afterlife are filled with disgust, and when other than Him are mentioned, suddenly they rejoice!

[Sūrah az-Zumar: 45]

They are excessive concerning the shaykh of the path, and they believe that he cures the sick, despite the fact that Allāh (ﷻ) mentioned the statement of 'Ibrāhīm (ﷺ) in the Noble Qur'ān:

﴿ وَإِذَا مَرِضْتُ فَهُوَ يَشْفِينِ ﴿٨٠﴾ ﴾

And when I am ill, it is He who cures me.

[Sūrah ash-Shu'arā': 80]

And there is the story of the believing child who used to supplicate for the sick, so Allāh (ﷻ) would cure them. When the companion of the king said, "You can have this money if you cure me!" The child said to him, "I don't cure anyone, Only Allāh cures. If you believe in Allāh, I will supplicate to Allāh for you, and He will cure you."

[Muslim]

With them, dhikr is made with the singular word "Allāh" thousands of times in their incantation, despite the fact that this type of dhikr with the word "Allāh" by itself has not been reported by the Messenger of Allāh (ﷺ), nor his companions or the generation after them, nor the imāms that reached the level of 'ijtihād. Rather, it is from the innovations of the Sufis because the word "Allāh" is a subject, and when a predicate does not come after it the speech becomes lacking. If a person were to call out the name 'Umar several times, so that we say to him, "What do you want from 'Umar?" and he does not respond with anything except "'Umar, 'Umar," we would say he is crazy and does not know what he's saying. As an evidence for making dhikr of Allāh with the singular word "Allāh," the Sufiyyah use the statement of Allāh (ﷻ):

﴿ قُلِ اللهُ ﴾

Say Allāh.

If they had read the speech that was before it, they would know that the meaning is "say Allāh revealed the Book," and the text of the full verse is:

﴿ وَمَا قَدَرُوا اللَّهَ حَقَّ قَدْرِهِ إِذْ قَالُوا مَا أَنزَلَ اللَّهُ عَلَىٰ بَشَرٍ مِّن شَيْءٍ ۗ قُلْ مَنْ أَنزَلَ الْكِتَابَ الَّذِي جَاءَ بِهِ مُوسَىٰ نُورًا وَهُدًى لِّلنَّاسِ ۖ تَجْعَلُونَهُ قَرَاطِيسَ تُبْدُونَهَا وَتُخْفُونَ كَثِيرًا ۖ وَعُلِّمْتُم مَّا لَمْ تَعْلَمُوا أَنتُمْ وَلَا آبَاؤُكُمْ ۖ قُلِ اللَّهُ ۖ ثُمَّ ذَرْهُمْ فِي خَوْضِهِمْ يَلْعَبُونَ ﴿٩١﴾ ﴾

And they did not estimate Allāh with a just estimation when they said Allāh has not sent down anything to mankind. Say, who sent down the book that Mūsā came with as a light and a guidance for mankind which you have made into pages, showing some of it and hiding much of it, and you were taught that which you nor your fathers knew? Say Allāh, then leave them to play in their vain discussions.

[Sūrah al-An'ām: 91]

This means to say that Allāh (ﷻ) revealed the book.

How I Moved to the Shādhilī Order

I met a shaykh from the Shādhilī order who had good manners and a good appearance. He visited me in my house, and I visited him in his. I liked his gentle speech, humility, and generosity, so I asked him to give me the daily portions of adhkār of the Shādhilī order. He gave me their private daily portions. There was also a Sufi lodge close to him where some of the youth would dhikr after the Friday prayer.

I visited him once in his house and saw a picture of many shuyukh from the Shādhilī order hanging on the wall. I reminded him of the prohibition that came concerning hanging pictures and he did not comply with it, despite the fact that the ḥadīth is clear and is not hidden to him. It is his statement (ﷺ), "Verily, the angels do not enter the house that has pictures in it." [Agreed upon by al-Bukhārī and Muslim] "The Messenger of Allāh (ﷺ) prohibited having images in the house and prohibited the man from making them." [Reported by at-Tirmidhī, and he said the ḥadīth is ḥasan ṣaḥīḥ.]

After about a year, I wanted to visit the shaykh while I was on my way to perform 'Umrah. He invited me, my son, and my friend to dinner. After finishing, he said to me, "Would you like to listen to anything from religious anashīd from these youths?" I said yes, so he commanded the youth that were around him—and they had beautiful beards on their faces—to recite. So, in one voice, they began to recite a nashīd, the gist of which was:

Whoever worships Allāh desiring His Paradise or fearing His Fire, then he has worshipped an idol.

Thus, I said to them, "Allāh mentioned a verse in the Qur'ān where he praised the prophets, saying:

﴿ إِنَّهُمْ كَانُوا يُسَارِعُونَ فِي الْخَيْرَاتِ وَيَدْعُونَنَا رَغَبًا وَرَهَبًا ۖ وَكَانُوا لَنَا خَاشِعِينَ ۝ ﴾

Verily, they used to rush to do good deeds, and supplicate to Us with hope and fear, and they used to humble themselves before us.

[Sūrah al-'Anbiyā': 90]

The shaykh said to me, "This nashīd that they recite is by the saint 'Abdul Ghanī an-Nābalusī!" I said, "And is the speech of the shaykh given precedence over the speech of Allāh, while it is a contradiction of it?!" One of the reciters said, "Our leader, 'Alī (☺) said, 'The one who worships Allāh hoping for His Paradise has worshipped with the worship of the businessmen.'" I said to him, "In which book did you find this statement by our leader 'Alī? And is it authentic?" He remained silent. I said to him, "Is it fathomable that 'Alī (☺) would oppose the Qur'ān while he is from the companions of the Messenger of Allāh (☺) and from those who have been given glad tidings of Paradise?" Then I turned to my friend, saying to him, "Allāh, the Most High, mentioned from the description of the believers, praising them:

﴿ تَتَجَافَىٰ جُنُوبُهُمْ عَنِ الْمَضَاجِعِ يَدْعُونَ رَبَّهُمْ خَوْفًا وَطَمَعًا ۝ ﴾

Their sides forsake their beds, while they call to their Lord in fear and hope.

[Sūrah as-Sajdah: 16]

They were not convinced, so I left off debating with them and went to the mosque for the prayer. One of the youths from them caught up to me, and said, "We're with you, and the truth is with you, but we aren't able to speak and refute the shaykh!" I said to him, "Why do you all not speak the truth?" He said, "He'll remove us from the housing if we speak." This is a general point of beginning for the Sufi, for the shuyukh of Sufism advise the students not to oppose the shaykh, no matter how much he errs. They say a famous statement, "No murīd who said to his shaykh 'Why?' has been successful!" This ignores the statement of the Messenger (ﷺ), "All of the children of Ādam err, and the best of those who err are those who repent." [The ḥadīth is ḥasan and reported by Aḥmed and at-Tirmidhī.] It also ignores the statement of Imām Mālik (ﷺ), "Everyone's statement is accepted or rejected except for the Messenger (ﷺ)."

THE SITTING OF THE SALUTATIONS

I went with some of the mashaykh to one of the mosques to attend this sitting, so we entered a dhikr circle. They were dancing, holding each other's hands, swaying, and going up and down, saying, "Allāh, Allāh..." Each person from the circle would go into the middle and point with his hands to those present to make them increase in movement and swaying. My turn came, and the head of the circle pointed at me to go into the middle to increase them in their movement and dancing. One of the mashaykh that were with me excused me and said to the head of the circle, "Leave him, he's weak," because he knows that I do not like the likes of these actions, and he saw me still and unmoving. So, their head left me alone and excused me from the middle of the circle. I heard poetry from beautiful voices, but they were not free from seeking aid and assistance from other than Allāh (ﷻ)! I noticed that the women would sit on an elevated place and watch the men, and there was a young woman from them who was uncovered, her hair and legs were showing, as were her hands and neck. I detested that in my heart. At the end of the sitting, I said to the head of the circle, "There is a young woman above us who is uncovered. If you reminded her, along with the rest of the women, of wearing the hijab in the mosque, it would be a good action." He said to me, "We don't give reminders to the women, nor do we tell them anything!" I said to him, "Why?" He said, "If we advise them, they won't come to attend the sittings of dhikr!" I said to myself, "There is no might or power except by Allāh! What is this dhikr in which the women are uncovered and are not advised by anyone? Would the Messenger (ﷺ) be pleased with this, while he is the one who said, 'Whoever from amongst you sees an evil then let him change it with his hand, and if he is not able to, then with his tongue, and if he is not able to, then with his heart, and that is the weakest of faith.'" [Muslim]

THE QĀDIRĪYYAH ORDER

One of the shuyukh of the path invited me, along with my shaykh that I studied grammar and tafsīr with, so we went to his house. After we ate dinner, those present stood doing dhikr, jumping, swaying, and saying, "Allāh, Allāh." I was standing with them, not moving, then I sat on a chair until the first part had ended. I saw the sweat pour from them, and they came with a towel to remove the sweat. Because the time came close to the middle of the night, I left them and went to my house. The next day, I met with one of those who sat with them. He used to teach with me. I said to him, "How long did you all remain in that condition?" He said, "Until two o'clock in the morning, when we went to our houses to sleep!" I said to him, "And the Fajr prayer, when did you all pray it?" He responded, "We didn't pray it on time. It passed us by."

I said to myself, "Maa shaa Allāh upon this dhikr that causes the morning prayer to be wasted!" (Note: He made this statement out of bewilderment and disapproval.) I remembered the statement of 'Ā'ishah (🌸) as she described the Messenger of Allāh (🌸). She said, "He used to sleep the first half of the night and stay awake the last half." [Agreed upon by al-Bukhārī and Muslim] Those Sufis do the opposite. They stay up the first half of the night with innovation and dancing, and they sleep the last half of it to let the Fajr prayer pass them by. Allāh (ﷻ) said:

﴿ فَوَيْلٌ لِّلْمُصَلِّينَ ﴿٤﴾ الَّذِينَ هُمْ عَن صَلَاتِهِمْ سَاهُونَ ﴿٥﴾ ﴾

So, woe unto those performers of the prayers, who delay their prayer from their stated fixed times.

[Sūrah al-Mā'ūn: 4-5]

This means they delay them from their fixed times. The Messenger of Allāh (ﷺ) said, "The two supererogatory units of prayer before Fajr are better than the world and everything in it." [Reported by at-Tirmidhī, and al-Albānī declared it to be authentic in *Ṣaḥīḥ al-Jāmi'*.]

CLAPPING DURING REMEMBRANCE

I was in a mosque and a dhikr circle was established after the Friday prayer, so I sat looking at them. One of them began to clap with his hands to make the singing and ecstasy increase. I gestured to him that this is prohibited and impermissible, but he did not stop clapping. When they finished, I advised him, but he did not accept it. I met with him after a period of time to remind him that this clapping is from the actions of the polytheists when Allāh (ﷻ) said about them:

﴿ وَمَا كَانَ صَلَاتُهُمْ عِندَ الْبَيْتِ إِلَّا مُكَاءً وَتَصْدِيَةً ﴿٣٥﴾ ﴾

And their prayer at the House (i.e., the Ka'bah) was not but whistling and clapping.

[Sūrah an-'Anfāl: 35]

He said to me, "But Shaykh so and so declared it to be permissible!" I said to myself, "These people, the statement of Allāh (ﷻ) applies to them."

﴿ اتَّخَذُوا أَحْبَارَهُمْ وَرُهْبَانَهُمْ أَرْبَابًا مِّن دُونِ اللَّهِ وَالْمَسِيحَ ابْنَ مَرْيَمَ ﴿٣١﴾ ﴾

They took their Rabbis and monks as lords besides Allāh, as well as the Messiah, the son of Maryam.

[Sūrah at-Tawbah: 31]

When 'Ady ibn Ḥātim aṭ-Ṭā'ī (رضي الله عنه) heard this verse, and he was a Christian before he embraced Islām, he said, "Oh Messenger of Allāh! Verily, we didn't worship them!" So, he (ﷺ) said to him, "Did they not declare permissible that which Allāh made impermissible, so you all also claimed it to be permissible? And declare impermissible that which Allāh made permissible, so you all also claimed it to be impermissible?" He said, "Rather, we did." The Prophet (ﷺ) said, "That was your worship of them." [Ḥasan, reported by at-Tirmidhī and al-Bayhaqī]

I attended another dhikr circle in a mosque, and the singer was clapping during the remembrance. After it ended, I said to him, "Your voice is beautiful, but this clapping you did is impermissible." He said to me, "The tune of singing isn't complete without clapping, and a shaykh that is bigger than you saw me and didn't criticize me!" Those who attend their dhikr circles notice that they practice deviation concerning the names of Allāh (ﷻ) and say, "Allāh, ah, hiya, huwa, yā huwa." This alteration and warping are impermissible. They will be brought to account for it on the Day of Judgement.

Hooking with Skewers

There is a Sufi lodge close to our house, I went there to see their dhikr. After the 'Ishā' prayer, the reciters came, and they had shaved faces. In one voice, they began to sway and repeat a line of poetry that says, "Give us a cup of wine, and fill up our vessels." The head of their circle would repeat this line by himself, then the others would repeat after him in a way that was like a group of singers and musicians! They were not shy about mentioning alcohol in the mosque that was made for the prayer and for the Qur'ān. Wine is alcohol, and Allāh (ﷻ) made alcohol impermissible in His Book. The Messenger (ﷺ) also forbade it in prophetic narrations.

Then, they began to beat drums intensely. One of them came up—he was old—and he took off his shirt. Then, he shouted at the top of his voice, "Oh Grandfather!" and he intended by that seeking aid from one of his dead grandparents who were from the sons of the Rifā'iyah order, because they were famous for doing this! Then, he took a metal skewer and stuck it in his flesh, while shouting "Oh grandfather!" A man wearing a military uniform with a shaved face came. He took a glass cup and began to bite it with his teeth! I said to myself, "If this soldier was truthful, why didn't he go to the Jews and fight them instead of breaking a cup with his teeth?" The year was 1967 AD when the Jews invaded a large part of the Arab lands. The Arabic armies had been defeated and lost the war, while this soldier was amongst them and did not do anything. And on top of that, he had a shaved face.

Some people think that this action is a miracle, and they do not know that this is from the work of the devils that gather around them and aid them upon their misguidance. This is because they turned away from the Remembrance of Allāh (ﷻ) and committed polytheism when they sought aid from their grandfathers, attesting to His a (ﷻ) statement:

﴿ وَمَن يَعْشُ عَن ذِكْرِ الرَّحْمَٰنِ نُقَيِّضْ لَهُ شَيْطَانًا فَهُوَ لَهُ قَرِينٌ ﴿٣٦﴾
وَإِنَّهُمْ لَيَصُدُّونَهُمْ عَنِ السَّبِيلِ وَيَحْسَبُونَ أَنَّهُم مُّهْتَدُونَ ﴿٣٧﴾ ﴾

And whoever blinds himself and turns away from the remembrance of the Most Merciful, We appoint

to him a devil to be a companion for him. And verily, they hinder them from the Path of Allāh, and they think that they are guided!

[Sūrah az-Zukhruf: 36-37]

Allāh (ﷻ) makes the devils subservient to them to increase them in misguidance, due to the statement of Allāh (ﷻ):

﴿ قُلْ مَن كَانَ فِي الضَّلَالَةِ فَلْيَمْدُدْ لَهُ الرَّحْمَٰنُ مَدًّا ﴿٧٥﴾ ﴾

Say, whoever is in misguidance, the Most Merciful will increase him in it.

[Sūrah Maryam: 75]

It is not strange that the devils help them and make them capable of doing that, just as has been witnessed. Those who went to India, such as the traveler Ibn Baṭūṭah and other than them, saw the Zoroastrians do more than this!

This matter is not a matter of a miracle or sainthood. Rather, hooking with skewers and other than it is from the works of the devils who have gathered around the singing and music, which is from the musical instrument of the devil. Most of those who do these actions commit sins; rather, they even commit polytheism openly. So how can they be from the allies of Allāh and people of miracles? Allāh (ﷻ) says:

﴿ أَلَا إِنَّ أَوْلِيَاءَ اللَّهِ لَا خَوْفٌ عَلَيْهِمْ وَلَا هُمْ يَحْزَنُونَ ﴿٦٢﴾ الَّذِينَ آمَنُوا وَكَانُوا يَتَّقُونَ ﴿٦٣﴾ ﴾

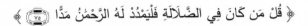

Verily, for the allies of Allāh there will be no fear, nor will they be sad, those who believe and fear Allāh.

[Sūrah Yūnūs: 62-63]

So, the ally of Allāh is the believer who fears Allāh (ﷻ), who distances himself from polytheism and sins, and seeks aid from Allāh, alone, in hardship and ease. And a miracle may come to him naturally, without seeking it and being famous in front of the people.

Shaykh al-Islām ibn Taymiyyah mentioned about the actions of the likes of these people and other than them. He said, "... And these actions do not happen for them when they read Qur'ān or pray because these are legislated actions of worship that are from faith, and they drive the devils away. Those actions that they do are innovated acts of worship that are based in polytheism. They are from the devils and philosophy, and they attract the devils."

That which is strange is that a person who was affected by the Sufi ideology, and his name is Sa'īd Ḥawā, was deceived by this falsehood. He wrote about it and called to studying the Rifā'iyah path. He narrated an occurrence that he had heard of and said of it, "A Christian man told me that a man stabbed him with a skewer in his stomach, so it exited from his back!" Then, he said, "And it might be that the person of this miracle is corrupt, so it's the miracle of his grandfather!" [Refer to the book *Our Spiritual Upbringing*, pg. 74.] The book takes the report of the miracle of a Christian man, and he might be lying. And do miracles happen for corrupt people? And since when are miracles inherited? Miracles are for the pious and the allies of Allāh (ﷻ). They are not inherited, nor are they for corrupt people. When something outside of the norm happens for a corrupt person, it is not called a miracle as Sa'īd Ḥawā claimed; rather, it is a gradual attraction to increase him in misguidance. And I have already mentioned that the Zoroastrians do actions more severe than hooking with skewers!

A Salafī man asked one of those charlatans who hook themselves with skewers to stick a safety pin into his eye. He refused and feared doing so. This points to the fact that they enter a specific type of skewer into their flesh. Those who used to do the likes of these actions—and then repented from them—speak about the blood that pours from them, and they wash off the blood after that.

An honest Muslim informed me that he saw a soldier stab himself with an iron skewer of a specific type, and he saw blood pour from the place the skewer was inserted. When he took him to his commanding officer, the officer said to him, "We're going to beat your legs with a rifle. So, if you are truthful, then be patient and stomach it." When they began to hit him, the soldier started to cry, shout, wail, and seek aid. He did not bear the beating, and the other soldiers began to laugh at him.

In Summary

The Messenger of Allāh (ﷺ) did not do it, nor did the companions of the Prophet (ﷺ), nor the generation after them, nor the Imāms of jurisprudence. If there were any good in it, they would have preceded us in it. However, it is from the actions of the polytheist innovators who came later and sought aid from the devils. The Messenger of Allāh (ﷺ) warned us from these innovations and said, “Be warned of newly invented matters. For verily, every newly invented matter is an innovation, and every innovation is misguidance, and every misguidance is in the Fire.” [Authentic, reported by an-Nasā'ī] The actions of these innovators are rejected, due to his (ﷺ) statement, “Whoever does an action which is not in accordance with what we are upon will be rejected.” [Muslim] These innovators seek assistance from the dead and the devils. This is from the polytheism that Allāh (ﷻ) warned against by His statement:

﴿ إِنَّهُ مَن يُشْرِكْ بِاللَّهِ فَقَدْ حَرَّمَ اللَّهُ عَلَيْهِ الْجَنَّةَ وَمَأْوَاهُ النَّارُ ۖ وَمَا لِلظَّالِمِينَ مِنْ أَنصَارٍ ﴿٧٢﴾ ﴾

Verily, whoever associates others with Allāh (in worship), then Allāh has forbidden for him the Paradise, and his abode is the Fire. And there are no helpers for the oppressors.

[Sūrah al-Mā'idah: 72]

And the Prophet (ﷺ) said, "Whoever dies while he supplicates to other than Allāh enters the Fire." [Sūrah al-Bukhārī]

Whoever believes as they have believed, or aids them, then they are from them.

The Mawlawī Order

They used to have a special Sufi lodge in my country called a Mawlawīyyah. It is a big mosque in which the daily prayers are prayed. There are a large number of the dead in it, and they have a fence around them. Raised, decorated stones were built above the graves. Verses from the Qur'ān are written upon them, along with the name of the person in the grave and lines of poetry. This group used to hold a ḥaḍrah (sitting where incantations are done) every Friday, or at events, and wear a long fez made of grey wool called a kallākh. They would also use a flute and other musical instruments during dhikr that could be heard from afar. I watched one of them stand in the middle of the circle, and he spun around many times, not moving from his spot. They would bow their heads when seeking aid from their shaykh, Jalāl al-Dīn ar-Rūmī, and other than him.

The strange thing is that the mosques in many of the Muslim lands, including this mosque, have the dead buried in them in imitation of the Jews and the Christians. The Messenger of

Allāh (ﷺ) said, "May the curse of Allāh be upon the Jews and the Christians. They took the graves of their prophets as places of worship." This is a warning against that which they did. [al-Bukhārī]

Praying to the graves is prohibited due to his (ﷺ) statement, "Do not sit on the graves, and do not pray to them." [Muslim and Aḥmed]

As for building on the graves, such as shrines, domes, and walls, writing upon them and painting them; listen to the prohibition of the Messenger (ﷺ). "He forbade from plastering the graves and from building upon them." [Muslim]. In another narration, "He prohibited from writing anything on the graves." [Reported by at-Tirmidhī and al-Hākim, adh-Dhahabī agreed with them.]

As for their usage of musical instruments in mosques and during dhikr, it is from the innovations of the later Sufis. The Messenger of Allāh (ﷺ) declared music to be impermissible with his statement, "Verily, there will be from my nation people who claim fornication, silk, alcohol, and musical instruments to be permissible." [Reported by al-Bukhārī without its chain of narration; 'Abū Dāwūd, Shaykh al-Albānī, and other than them declared the narration to be authentic.] The exception to the prohibition on musical instruments is the duff on the day of 'Eīd and at marriages for the women.

They used to go from mosque to mosque to establish what is called an-nawiyyah, which is dhikr with musical instruments. They used to stay up late into the night and cause the people in the area to hear the abominable musical instruments.

I used to know one of them. He used to dress his son in the sun hats that the disbelievers wear. I secretly took it and tore it up. This Sufi became upset due to the tearing of the sun hat, and he angrily chastised me. I told him, "My sense of honor and jealousy for your child who wears the clothing of disbelievers overtook me," and I apologized to him. He used to hang a banner in his office on which was written, "Oh our honorable protector, Jalāl ad-Dīn." I said to him, "How do you call out to this shaykh that cannot hear or answer?" He was silent.

And this is a summary of the Mawlawī order.

A Strange Lesson from a Sufi Shaykh

One time, I went with one of the Sufi shuyukh to a class in one of the mosques. A number of the teachers and mashaykh gathered for it, and they were reading from a book named *Wisdoms by Ibn Ajeebah.* The class was about cultivation of the soul with the Sufiyyah. One of them read in the aforementioned book a strange story.

A Sufi entered a bathhouse to bathe. When he left the bathhouse, he stole the towel that the owner gives to the one who bathes. He left the edge of it uncovered so the people could see it and scold and slander him. This was to belittle himself and cultivate it upon the Sufi path. Indeed, when the Sufi left the bathhouse, the owner of the bathhouse caught up to him and saw the edge of the towel under his thobe. The owner scolded him, was bad to him, and the people listened to him and saw this Sufi shaykh that stole the towel from the bathhouse. The people rained down slander, insults, and other than that; and they took a bad image from this Sufi!

Another Sufi wanted to cultivate his soul and belittle it, so he carried a bag around his neck and filled it with nutmeg fruit. He went to the market, and every time a child passed by him, he would say to him, "Spit in my face so I can give you a nutmeg fruit." It is a fruit that the children love, so the child would spit in his face, and he would give him a nutmeg fruit. And like this, the spit from the children came in succession on the face of the shaykh, desiring to take the nutmeg fruit, while the Sufi shaykh was happy. When I heard these two stories, I almost burst with rage and my chest became tightened from this corrupt cultivation that Islām is free from. Islām ennobled mankind by the statement of Allāh (ﷻ):

﴿ وَلَقَدْ كَرَّمْنَا بَنِي آدَمَ وَحَمَلْنَاهُمْ فِي الْبَرِّ وَالْبَحْرِ ٧٠ ﴾

And We have certainly honored the children of Ādam and carried them on the land and sea.

[Sūrah al-'Isrā': 70]

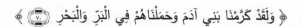

After the lesson, I said to the shaykh who was with me, "This is the Sufi path of cultivating the soul! Is its cultivation by impermissible theft that the Divine legislation has decreed with cutting off the hand of the thief? Or is it by being belittled while the young do the most despicable of actions? Verily, Islām rejects these actions, and the sound intellect that Allāh (ﷻ) has honored mankind with rejects them! Are these from the wisdoms that the shaykh named his book *Wisdoms by Ibn Ajeebah*?!

And from that which is befitting to be mentioned is that this shaykh who leads the class has many followers and students. Once, the shaykh announced that he wanted to do Ḥajj, so the students went to sign up with him and write their names to accompany the shaykh on Ḥajj. Even the women began signing up, and it is likely they needed to sell their jewelry to do that. The number of people who wanted to go reached a very high number, and he gathered a tremendous amount of money. Then, he announced that he was not able to go on Ḥajj, and he didn't return the money to the people. Rather, he kept it for himself by impermissible means! The statement of Allāh (ﷻ) bears true upon him:

﴿ يَا أَيُّهَا الَّذِينَ آمَنُوا إِنَّ كَثِيرًا مِّنَ الْأَحْبَارِ وَالرُّهْبَانِ لَيَأْكُلُونَ أَمْوَالَ
النَّاسِ بِالْبَاطِلِ وَيَصُدُّونَ عَن سَبِيلِ اللَّهِ ﴿٣٤﴾ ﴾

O you who believe! Verily, many of the rabbis and monks devour the wealth of the people unjustly and avert them from the Path of Allāh.

[Sūrah at-Tawbah: 34]

I heard one of his followers—who is from the wealthy and had worked with the shaykh—say about him, "He is the biggest liar and the biggest scam artist!"

Dhikr in the Mosques of the Sufis

Once, I attended a dhikr sitting of the Sufis in the mosque of the neighborhood that I live in, and a man from them with a beautiful voice began to sing anashīd and poetry for them during the remembrance. I remember him saying, "Oh men of the unseen, help us, save us, give us victory ..." to the end of all the other requests for help and requesting needs from the dead that do not hear. Even if they could hear, they would not answer them, and they are not able to benefit themselves, let alone other than them. The Qur'ān alluded to them in the statement:

﴿ وَالَّذِينَ تَدْعُونَ مِن دُونِهِ مَا يَمْلِكُونَ مِن قِطْمِيرٍ ﴿١٣﴾ إِن تَدْعُوهُمْ لَا
يَسْمَعُوا دُعَاءَكُمْ وَلَوْ سَمِعُوا مَا اسْتَجَابُوا لَكُمْ ۖ وَيَوْمَ الْقِيَامَةِ يَكْفُرُونَ بِشِرْكِكُمْ ۚ
وَلَا يُنَبِّئُكَ مِثْلُ خَبِيرٍ ﴿١٤﴾ ﴾

Those who you call on other than Him do not even possess the membrane of a date seed. If you invoke them, they do not hear your supplication; and even if they heard, they would not answer you. And on the Day of Judgement, they will deny your association of them (as partners in worship alongside Allāh). And none can inform you like one who is Informed of all matters.

[Sūrah Fātir: 13-14]

The dhikr sitting ended and I exited. Then I said to the shaykh who was the imām of the mosque that participated in it, "This dhikr does not deserve to be called dhikr because I did not hear the remembrance of Allāh in it, nor seeking from Allāh, nor supplication of Him. I only heard supplication and calling to the men of the unseen. And who are the men of the unseen who are able to give us victory, save us, and help us?" The shaykh went silent. The biggest refutation of them is the statement of Allāh (ﷻ):

﴿ وَالَّذِينَ تَدْعُونَ مِن دُونِهِ لَا يَسْتَطِيعُونَ نَصْرَكُمْ وَلَا أَنفُسَهُمْ يَنصُرُونَ ١٩٧ ﴾

And those who you invoke besides Him are not able to help you, nor are they able to help themselves.

[Sūrah al-A'rāf: 197]

Another time, I went to a different mosque that had a large number of people in it, and there was a Sufi shaykh in the mosque who had followers. After the prayer, they began a dhikr circle, and began to jump and dance during the remembrance. They were shouting "Allāh, aah, hiya." The singer got close to the shaykh and began to dance in front of him and sway as if he was a female singer or dancer. He was acting seductively to his shaykh. Meanwhile, the shaykh was looking at him smiling and pleased with it. I used to visit this shaykh sometimes with my shaykh, and he was also a Sufi. Once, I visited him after he had returned from Ḥajj. We sat down to listen to him, and he began to speak about riding in a large, comfortable American car. This was when they took him from Makkah to Madinah. I said to myself, "What is the benefit in this speech? It was more befitting that he speak about the spiritual and social benefits of the Ḥajj and other than that, implementing the statement of Allāh (ﷻ):

﴿ لِّيَشْهَدُوا مَنَافِعَ لَهُمْ ﴾ ٢٨

That they may witness things that are of benefit for them

[Sūrah al-Ḥajj: 28]

How the Sufis Deal with the People

I bought a storefront from one of the students of the aforementioned Sufi shaykh and made it conditional that he pays on behalf of the renter it if the renter is ever late on rent, and he was pleased with that. After a while, the renter refused to pay rent. Thus, I returned to the previous owner who I bought the storefront from, and he refused to pay anything, claiming that he did not have enough to pay. After a few days, this Sufi went with his shaykh to Ḥajj. I was astonished, and I found out that he was a liar. I complained of the situation to some of the close students of the shaykh and told them about this man who cheated me and sold me a storefront whose renter does not pay rent. He did not do anything and said, "What can we do with him?" If he was just, he would have called him over and requested that he give the people their right.

I used to go repeatedly to this guarantor's place. He had a textile factory. One of the students of the shaykh used to sing poetry, sway, and dance in front of the shaykh. He saw me, and knew I was looking for his friend. I asked him to show me where he was, and I told him what his friend did. Instead of being just to me, he rained down obscene and lowly speech on me. I left him and said to myself, "These are the manners of the Sufis, and the Messenger (ﷺ) warned against them with his statement, 'There are four attributes that whoever has in them is a pure hypocrite, and whoever has one of them then an attribute of hypocrisy is in him. When he speaks, he lies, and when he promises, he breaks his promise, and when he makes an agreement he betrays it, and when he argues he uses foul speech." [Agreed upon by al-Bukhārī and Muslim]

HOW I WAS GUIDED TO MONOTHEISM

I used to read upon the shaykh with whom I studied the ḥadīth of Ibn 'Abbās (). It was statement of the Messenger of Allāh (), "When you ask, ask Allāh and when you seek help, seek help from Allāh." [Reported by at-Tirmidhī, and he said the ḥadīth is ḥasan ṣaḥīḥ.] I liked the explanation of an-Nawawī when he said, "Then, if there is a need that one asks for, and it's not the norm that it happens at the hands of His creation, such as asking for guidance or knowledge, and curing the sick and attaining good health, he asks his Lord for that. As for asking the creation and relying upon them, then it is blameworthy."

I told the shaykh that this ḥadīth, and its explanation, are indicative of the impermissibility of seeking aid from other than Allāh. He said to me, "Rather, it is permissible!" I said, "And what is your evidence?" The shaykh became angry and shouted, saying, "My aunt says, 'Oh Shaykh Sa'ad'" He is buried in the mosque, and she seeks aid from him. I ask her, "Oh auntie, does Shaykh Sa'ad benefit you?" She says, "I invoke him, so he enters upon Allāh and acts as an intercessor for me!!"

I said to him, "You are a man who is a scholar. You have spent your life reading books, then you take your beliefs from your ignorant aunt!" He said to me, "You have Wahhābī thoughts. You go to 'Umrah, and you come back with Wahhābī books!!!"

I used to not know anything about Wahhābīyyah, except what I would hear from the mashaykh. They say about them, "Wahhābīs oppose the people. They do not believe in the allies of Allāh or their miracles. They don't love the Messenger (ﷺ)," and other than that from the untrue accusations! I said to myself, "If the Wahhābīs believe in seeking aid from Allāh, alone, and that Allāh, alone, is The One who cures, then it is binding upon me to get to know them. I asked about them, so they said, "They have a place where they gather on Thursday nights to give lessons in tafsīr, ḥadīth, and Islāmic jurisprudence." So, I went to them with my children and some of the cultured youth. We entered a big room and sat waiting for the lesson to begin. After a period of time, an older shaykh entered. He said to all of us, "As-Salāmu 'Alaykum" and shook our hands, starting at his right. Then, he sat on his chair, and no one stood up for him. I said to myself, "This shaykh is humble. He doesn't like people to stand for him."

The Shaykh started the class with his statement, "Verily, all praise and thanks is for Allāh. We praise Him, seek His aid, and seek His forgiveness ...” to the end of the speech that the Messenger (ﷺ) would begin his sermons and lessons with. He spoke the proper Arabic language, and would mention aḥadīth, and clarify their authenticity and narrators. He sent salutations on the Prophet (ﷺ) every time he would mention his name. At the end, questions written on pieces of paper were posed to him, and he would answer with evidence from the Qur’ān and sunnah. Some of those present would converse with him, and he would not turn any questioner away. At the end of the class, he said, “All praise be to Allāh for us being Muslims and Salafīs.” Salafīs are those who follow the righteous predecessors, the Messenger (ﷺ) and his companions. Some of the people say that we are Wahhābīs. This is insulting by name calling and Allāh (ﷻ) had prohibited this with his statement:

﴿ وَلَا تَنَابَزُوا بِالْأَلْقَابِ ﴿١١﴾ ﴾

And do not insult one another by calling names.

[Sūrah al-Ḥujurāt: 11]

In the past, they accused Imām Ash-Shāfi‘ī of being a Rāfiḍī, so he refuted them, saying:

“If Rafḍ is loving the family of Muḥammad (ﷺ), then let mankind and the jinn bear witness that I am a Rāfiḍī.”

And we respond to those who accuse us of being Wahhābīs with the statement of one of the poets:

"If the one who follows Aḥmed is a Wahhābī, then I affirm that I am a Wahhābī."

When the lesson ended, we left with some of the youth that were impressed by his knowledge and humility. I heard one of them say, "That's the real shaykh!"

THE MEANING OF WAHHĀBĪ

The enemies of monotheism use the word Wahhābī against the monotheists, associating them to Muḥammad ibn 'Abdul Wahhāb. If they were truthful, they would have said Muḥammadī, associating them to his name, Muḥammad (ﷺ). But Allāh (ﷻ) decreed that the word Wahhābī associates to al-Wahhāb, and it is a name from the beautiful names of Allāh (ﷻ). So, while the Sufi is affiliated to a group of people who wear wool, the Wahhābī is affiliated to al-Wahhāb. And the name al-Wahhāb is from the names of Allāh (ﷻ), who granted him monotheism and allowed him to call to Him, by the success from Allāh (ﷻ).

DEBATE WITH THE SUFI SHAYKH

When the shaykh that I used to study with found out that I went to the Salafīs and listened to Shaykh Muḥammad Nāṣir ad-Dīn al-

Albānī, he became extremely angry because he feared that I would leave him and turn against him. After a period of time, a person who lives beside the mosque came to attend the lesson with us in the mosque after the Maghrib prayer. He began to narrate to us that he heard one of the Sufi mashaykh say in one of his lessons, "A student of his had difficulty with his wife getting pregnant and giving birth, so he called out to a small shaykh for help (and he intended himself by this). She gave birth and the hardship was removed from her. The shaykh that we study with said to him, "And what's wrong with this?" The man said to him, "This is polytheism." The shaykh said to him, "Shut up, you don't know what polytheism is. You are a blacksmith, and we are mashaykh. We have knowledge, and we know more than you." Then the shaykh got up and went to his room, and he came back with the book *Al-Adhkār* by an-Nawawī. He began to read the story of Ibn 'Umar. In the story, it states that his leg went numb, and he said, "Oh Muḥammad!" "So did he commit polytheism?" he asked. The man replied, "That ḥadīth is inauthentic." The shaykh shouted angrily, "You don't know the authentic from the inauthentic! We are scholars. We know that!" Then, the shaykh turned to me and said, "If this man attends the lesson again, I'm going to kill him!" We left the mosque, and the man requested that I send my son with him to get the book *Al-Adhkār* with the commentary of Shaykh 'Abdul Qādir al-Arnā'ūṭ. He came with it and gave it to me. Sure enough, the commentator said that the story was inauthentic. The next day, my son gave the shaykh the book and he found out that the story was inauthentic, but he did not admit to his mistake. He said, "This is in the virtue of actions, the weak aḥadīth are accepted in it!" I say, "Verily, this is not from the virtue of actions as the shaykh had claimed. Rather, this is about creed, in which it is not permissible to accept the weak aḥadīth, with full knowledge that Imām Muslim and other than him hold the opinion of not accepting a weak ḥadīth in virtue of actions. Those who say that it is permissible to accept weak aḥadīth in the virtue of actions from the later scholars view its permissibility only with a number of conditions that are rare to find. Also, this is a story and not a ḥadīth. It is not from the virtue of actions; rather, it is from the foundations of beliefs as has been mentioned previously. The next day, we came to the lesson, and after the Shaykh ended the prayer, he left the mosque. He did not stay as was the norm for him to do after the lesson.

The shaykh tried to convince me that seeking aid from other than Allāh (ﷻ) is permissible, like tawassul (drawing close to Allāh by actions of worship). He began to give me some books, and from them was the book *Destroying Lies About the Matter of Tawassul* by Zāhid al-Kawtharī. I read it and found that he claims seeking aid from other than Allāh (ﷻ) is permissible. He came to the ḥadīth, "When you ask, ask Allāh, and when you seek aid, seek aid from Allāh." [Reported by at-Tirmidhī and he said it is ḥasan ṣaḥīḥ.] Al-Kawtharī said about it, "Its chains of narration are weak," and due to this he did not accept it. However, it is known that an-Nawawī mentioned the ḥadīth in his book *Forty Ḥadīth of An-Nawawī*, and it is the nineteenth ḥadīth. Imām at-Tirmidhī reported the ḥadīth, and he said that it was ḥasan ṣaḥīḥ. An-Nawawī and other than them from the scholars agreed with this. Therefore, I was astounded by al-Kawtharī, how he rejected the ḥadīth because it did not agree with his creed. I increased in hatred of him and his beliefs, while I increased in love of the Salafīs and their beliefs that prohibit seeking aid from other than Allāh (ﷻ) due to the aforementioned ḥadīth and the statement of Allāh (ﷻ):

﴿ وَلَا تَدْعُ مِن دُونِ اللَّهِ مَا لَا يَنفَعُكَ وَلَا يَضُرُّكَ ۖ فَإِن فَعَلْتَ فَإِنَّكَ إِذًا مِّنَ الظَّالِمِينَ ﴿١٠٦﴾ ﴾

And do not call upon other than Allāh any that will not benefit you or harm you, and if you did so, you will certainly be from the oppressors (i.e., the polytheists).

[Sūrah Yūnūs: 106]

Also, the statement of the Prophet (ﷺ), "Supplication, it is worship." [Reported by at-Tirmidhī, and he said it is ḥasan ṣaḥīḥ.]

When my shaykh saw that I was not convinced by the books he gave me, he boycotted me and spread about me, "He is a Wahhābī. Beware of him." I said to myself, "They said about our leader Muḥammad (ﷺ) that he was a sorcerer or insane. They said about Imām Ash-Shāfi'ī that he was a Rāfiḍī, so he refuted them, saying,

"If Rafḍ is loving the family of Muḥammad (ﷺ), then let mankind and the jinn bear witness that I am a Rāfiḍī."

They called one of the monotheists a Wahhābī, so he refuted them, saying:

"If following Aḥmed is Wahhābīyyah, then I affirm that I am a Wahhābī. I negate partners with Allāh (in worship), so I have no Lord except the Unrivalled, the Granter. I do not have hope in a dome, nor an idol, nor does a grave have control of any means."

I praise and thank Allāh, the One who has guided me to monotheism and the creed of the righteous predecessors. I began to call to monotheism and spread it amongst the people, taking the best of mankind (ﷺ) as an example, who began his call to monotheism in Makkah for 13 years. He and his companions patiently bore harm until monotheism had spread, and a nation of monotheism was established by the favor of Allāh (ﷻ).

THE SUFI MASHAYKH ON MONOTHEISM

I published a pamphlet comprised of four pages titled "Lā ilāha illa Allāh (there is no deity worthy of worship but Allāh) Muḥammad is the Messenger of Allāh, You Alone we worship and You Alone we ask for help, when you ask, ask Allāh, and when you seek aid, seek aid from Allāh). I explained their meanings and used the statement of an-Nawawī as evidence in the explanation of the ḥadīth, as well as the statements of other than him from the scholars who called to monotheism. Just so the mashaykh would not say about the pamphlet that it is a Wahhābī pamphlet, I mentioned the statement of Shaykh 'Abdul Qādir al-Jīlānī from his book *The Divine Victory*, "Ask Allāh and do not ask other than him, seek aid from Allāh and don't seek aid from other than him. Woe be to you! With what face will you meet Him tomorrow, while you conflict with Him in the worldly life, turning away from Him, rushing toward His creation, associating partners with Him in worship! You seek your needs from them and rely on them in the important matters! Remove the intercessors between you and Allāh, for your standing with them is madness. There is no dominion, nor power, nor wealth, nor might except for al-Ḥaqq. Be with al-Ḥaqq, without the creation (i.e., be with al-Ḥaqq by supplicating to Him without an intercessor from his creation)."

This is the gist of the small pamphlet comprised of four pages. The Ministry of Media allowed the publication of it, and 30,000 copies of it were printed. My son distributed a few of the copies and heard one of the mashaykh say, "This is a Wahhābī pamphlet." It reached a big shaykh in the land and he criticized it. He sought to meet with me, so I went to his house. This shaykh had studied with me in the Khaṣrawīyah school in Aleppo, and it is now called the Sharī'ah Secondary School. When I rang the bell, a girl came out. I said to her, "Muḥammad Zeno." She went inside and then returned. She told me, "He's coming to the school after a bit, so wait for him there." I sat at the barber shop next to his house until he came out. I caught up with him and said, "What do you want from me?" He said to me, "I don't want your pamphlet!" "Why?" I asked him. He replied, "We don't want it." When we reached the door of the school, I told him, "I'll enter the school with you, and read the treatise." He said, "I don't have time!" I said to him, "I've printed 30,000 copies and it costed a lot of money and effort. What do we do with them? Do we burn them?" He told me, "Yes, burn them!!" I said to myself, "I'm going to go to Shaykh Muḥammad as-Saqlini, who was my teacher in Ḥanafī fiqh. I went to him and said, "I have a small treatise and one of the mashaykh told me to burn it." He said, "Read it to me." I read it to him, and he said, "This treatise has the Qur'ān, the speech of Allāh in it, and the aḥadīth of the Messenger of Allāh (ﷺ) in it. How can we burn it?" I said to him, "May Allāh reward you with good. I will distribute it, and I won't burn it." After a period of time, I distributed it. I found the cultured youth to be receptive to it, to the point that I found someone who printed it and spread it in the Watār Library in Miskīyyah, in the city of Damascus. I praised and thanked Allāh (ﷻ) for having facilitated someone who printed and distributed this treatise for free to spread the benefit. I remembered the statement of Allāh (ﷻ):

﴿ يُرِيدُونَ أَن يُطْفِئُوا نُورَ اللَّهِ بِأَفْوَاهِهِمْ وَيَأْبَى اللَّهُ إِلَّا أَن يُتِمَّ نُورَهُ وَلَوْ كَرِهَ الْكَافِرُونَ ﴿٣٢﴾ هُوَ الَّذِي أَرْسَلَ رَسُولَهُ بِالْهُدَىٰ وَدِينِ الْحَقِّ لِيُظْهِرَهُ عَلَى الدِّينِ كُلِّهِ وَلَوْ كَرِهَ الْمُشْرِكُونَ ﴿٣٣﴾ ﴾

They want to extinguish the light of Allāh with their mouths, but Allāh does not allow except that His light be perfected, even if the disbelievers hate it. He is the One who sent His Messenger with the guidance and the true religion to make it superior over all religions, even if the polytheists hate it.

[Sūrah at-Tawbah: 32-33]

Then, I published this treatise in my book *The Methodology of the Saved Sect*. So, whoever wants to read over it, let him read that book and he will find it with the same headings that were previously mentioned.

One of the shaykhs gave me a book as a gift. It had in it the famous story of Tha'labah. When he wanted to print the book again, I advised him to return to the statements of the scholars, especially in the book *Al-Isābah fī 'Asmā As-Ṣaḥābah* by Ibn Ḥajar. For he and other than him had mentioned that it is not authentic. He did not accept the advice, and said to me, "You are zealous, leave off these matters!" I told him, "If I leave them off, I'll call to the monotheism that the Messenger (ﷺ) taught his cousin 'Abdullāh ibn 'Abbās when he was a child. The Messenger (ﷺ) said to him, "O young man, I will teach you some words. When you ask, ask

Allāh, and when you seek aid, seek aid from Allāh ..." to the end of the ḥadīth that an-Nawawī mentioned, and at-Tirmidhī said it is ḥasan ṣaḥīḥ. He told me, "We ask other than Allāh!" and rejected the ḥadīth with every bit of shamelessness and bad manners, opposing the statement of Allāh (ﷻ):

﴿ وَلَا تَدْعُ مِن دُونِ اللَّهِ مَا لَا يَنفَعُكَ وَلَا يَضُرُّكَ ۖ فَإِن فَعَلْتَ فَإِنَّكَ إِذًا مِّنَ الظَّالِمِينَ ﴿١٠٦﴾ ﴾

And do not call upon other than Allāh any that will not benefit you or harm you, and if you did so you will certainly be from the oppressors (i.e., the polytheists).

[Sūrah Yūnūs: 106]

A few years went by, and this shaykh who asks other than Allāh, one of his sons was murdered and two others were put in prison. He left his house and suddenly immigrated to another country. Allāh (ﷻ) decreed that I meet with this shaykh in the noble Masjid al-Ḥarām. I hoped that he had come to his senses and returned to Allāh (ﷻ), asking Him for protection and aid. I greeted him, and said, "If Allāh wills, we will return to our country, and Allāh will relieve us. So, it is upon us to turn to Allāh and ask him for aid and assistance; for He is the only One who is Capable of all things. What do you think?" He said to me, "There is differing in the matter." I asked him, "What differing? You are an imām of a mosque, and you read in every unit of your prayer:

﴿ إِيَّاكَ نَعْبُدُ وَإِيَّاكَ نَسْتَعِينُ ۝٥ ﴾

You, alone, we worship, and You, alone, we ask for help.

[Sūrah al-Fātiḥah: 5]

The Muslim repeats it in tens of times in his day, especially in his prayer," but this Naqshibandī Sufi shaykh did not retract his error. Rather, he persisted and began to debate, and considered it to be a matter that has differing in it to justify his erroneous stance! The polytheists that waged war against the Messenger of Allāh (ﷺ) used to invoke their saints in times of ease; but when they fell on hard times or calamities, they asked Allāh, alone, just as Allāh (ﷻ) said about them:

﴿ هُوَ الَّذِي يُسَيِّرُكُمْ فِي الْبَرِّ وَالْبَحْرِ ۖ حَتَّىٰ إِذَا كُنتُمْ فِي الْفُلْكِ وَجَرَيْنَ بِهِم بِرِيحٍ طَيِّبَةٍ وَفَرِحُوا بِهَا جَاءَتْهَا رِيحٌ عَاصِفٌ وَجَاءَهُمُ الْمَوْجُ مِن كُلِّ مَكَانٍ وَظَنُّوا أَنَّهُمْ أُحِيطَ بِهِمْ ۙ دَعَوُا اللَّهَ مُخْلِصِينَ لَهُ الدِّينَ لَئِنْ أَنجَيْتَنَا مِنْ هَٰذِهِ لَنَكُونَنَّ مِنَ الشَّاكِرِينَ ۝٢٢ ﴾

He is the one that causes you to travel by land and sea, until you are in ships sailing with a favorable wind, while they are happy with it; then comes a stormy wind and waves come from every place, and they think they are surrounded, they invoke

Allāh, making their worship solely for Him, saying "If You deliver us from this, we will certainly be from the thankful."

[Sūrah Yūnūs: 22]

And He (ﷻ) said about the polytheists:

﴿ ثُمَّ إِذَا مَسَّكُمُ الضُّرُّ فَإِلَيْهِ تَجْأَرُونَ ٥٣ ﴾

Then, when harm touches you, you cry out to Him for help.

[Sūrah an-Naḥl: 53]

One time, I entered upon a big shaykh who has students and followers. He gives sermons and is the imām of a big mosque. I began to speak with him about supplication being an act of worship, and it is not permissible except to supplicate to Allāh (ﷻ), alone. I gave him evidence from the Qur'ān, and it is His (ﷻ) statement:

﴿ قُلِ ادْعُوا الَّذِينَ زَعَمْتُم مِّن دُونِهِ فَلَا يَمْلِكُونَ كَشْفَ الضُّرِّ عَنكُمْ وَلَا تَحْوِيلًا ﴿٥٦﴾ أُولَٰئِكَ الَّذِينَ يَدْعُونَ يَبْتَغُونَ إِلَىٰ رَبِّهِمُ الْوَسِيلَةَ أَيُّهُمْ أَقْرَبُ وَيَرْجُونَ رَحْمَتَهُ وَيَخَافُونَ عَذَابَهُ ۚ إِنَّ عَذَابَ رَبِّكَ كَانَ مَحْذُورًا ٥٧ ﴾

Say, "Call upon those who you have claimed to be gods other than Him, for they do not possess the capability of removing harm from you or moving it to someone else. Those who they call on want a

means of access to their Lord, as to which of them would be the nearest, and they (i.e., those that they call on) hope for His mercy and fear His torment. Verily, the torment of Your Lord is something to be afraid of!

[Sūrah al-'Isrā': 56-57]

I said, "So, what is intended by His statement, 'Those who they call on ...'?" He said to me, "The idols." I told him, "That which is intended are the saints and righteous people." He told me, "We will return to *Tafsīr ibn Kathīr*." He reached his hand out to his bookshelf and took out *Tafsīr ibn Kathīr*. He found that Ibn Kathīr makes a large number of statements concerning the meaning of the verse, and that the most authentic of them is the narration that was reported by al-Bukhārī. It says, "A people from the jinn said that they used to be worshipped, and then they embraced Islām;" and in another narration, "There were people from mankind who used worship people from the jinn, so the jinn embraced Islām, and those humans remained upon their religion (i.e., worshipping the jinn)." [al-Bukhārī, vol. 3, pg. 46]

The shaykh said to me, "The truth is with you." I was happy with his admission and began to visit him frequently and sit in his room. One day, as I was with him, he shocked me and said to some people who were present, "The Wahhābīs are halfway disbelievers because they don't believe in the souls." I said to myself, "The shaykh has changed his opinion and feared for his position, so he lied upon the Wahhābīs." The Wahhābīs do not deny the belief in souls, because they are confirmed in the Qur'ān and aḥadīth. They deny that the soul is able to dispose of affairs, such as saving the oppressed person, aiding the living, benefiting them, or harming them. This is because it is major polytheism which the Qur'ān has mentioned regarding the dead. Allāh (ﷻ) says in His statement:

﴿ وَالَّذِينَ تَدْعُونَ مِن دُونِهِ مَا يَمْلِكُونَ مِن قِطْمِيرٍ ﴿١٣﴾ إِن تَدْعُوهُمْ لَا
يَسْمَعُوا دُعَاءَكُمْ وَلَوْ سَمِعُوا مَا اسْتَجَابُوا لَكُمْ ۖ وَيَوْمَ الْقِيَامَةِ يَكْفُرُونَ بِشِرْكِكُمْ ۚ
وَلَا يُنَبِّئُكَ مِثْلُ خَبِيرٍ ﴿١٤﴾ ﴾

Those who you call on other than Him do not even possess the membrane of a date seed. If you invoke them, they do not hear your supplication; and even if they heard, they would not answer you. And on the Day of Judgement, they will deny your association of them (as partners in worship alongside Allāh). And none can inform you like One who is Informed of all matters.

[Sūrah Fātir: 13-14]

These verses are clear in stating that the dead do not have dominion over anything, and that they don't hear the supplication of other than them. Even if they heard them, they would not be able to answer. And on the Day of Judgement, they will deny this polytheism as the verse clearly stated:

﴿ وَيَوْمَ الْقِيَامَةِ يَكْفُرُونَ بِشِرْكِكُمْ ﴿١٤﴾ ﴾

And on the Day of Judgement, they will deny your association of them (as partners in worship alongside Allāh).

[Sūrah Fātīr: 14]

ONLY ALLĀH KNOWS THE UNSEEN

I was with some of the Sufi mashaykh in the local mosque, studying the Qur'ān with them after Fajr, and all of them have the Noble Qur'ān memorized. As we were reciting the Qur'ān, we came by the statement of Allāh (ﷻ):

﴿ قُل لَّا يَعْلَمُ مَن فِي السَّمَاوَاتِ وَالْأَرْضِ الْغَيْبَ إِلَّا اللَّهُ ﴿٦٥﴾ ﴾

Say, "None in the heavens and the earth know the unseen except Allāh.

[Sūrah an-Naml: 65]

I told them, "Verily, this verse is a clear evidence that no one knows the unseen except Allāh." They stood against me and said, "The saints know the unseen!!" I said to them, "What is your evidence?" Every one of them began narrating stories that they heard from some people, that saint so and so informs of matters of the unseen! I said to them, "These stories could be lies, and they are not evidence; especially since they oppose the Qur'ān. How can you take them and leave the Qur'ān?!" But they were not convinced, and some of them began to shout, and anger overtook them. I did not find one of them who took the verse. Rather, they all agreed upon falsehood, and their evidence was mythical stories that they passed around without having any real basis. I left the mosque, and I did not attend their sitting the next day. I sat with children, reading the Qur'ān with them. It is better for me than sitting with people who have the Qur'ān memorized yet oppose that which is in it from beliefs, and they do not implement its rulings. It is obligatory upon the Muslim, when he sees the likes of them, to not sit with them, acting upon the statement of Allāh (ﷻ):

﴿وَإِمَّا يُنسِيَنَّكَ الشَّيْطَانُ فَلَا تَقْعُدْ بَعْدَ الذِّكْرَىٰ مَعَ الْقَوْمِ الظَّالِمِينَ ﴿٦٨﴾﴾

And if the devil causes you to forget, then do not sit with the wrongdoing people after the reminder.

[Sūrah al-An'ām: 68]

They are wrongdoers who associate servants with Allāh (ﷻ) in worship, who they claim know the affairs of the unseen. Allāh speaks to His Messenger (ﷺ) and commands him to say to the people:

﴿ قُل لَّا أَمْلِكُ لِنَفْسِي نَفْعًا وَلَا ضَرًّا إِلَّا مَا شَاءَ اللَّهُ ۚ وَلَوْ كُنتُ أَعْلَمُ الْغَيْبَ لَاسْتَكْثَرْتُ مِنَ الْخَيْرِ وَمَا مَسَّنِيَ السُّوءُ ۚ إِنْ أَنَا إِلَّا نَذِيرٌ وَبَشِيرٌ لِّقَوْمٍ يُؤْمِنُونَ ﴿١٨٨﴾ ﴾

Say, "I do not have dominion over benefit or harm for myself, except for that which Allāh wills. And if I knew the unseen, I would have amassed much wealth, and no harm would have touched me. Verily, I am only a warner and a bearer of glad tidings for a people who believe."

[Sūrah al-'A'rāf: 188]

Those previously mentioned people who have memorized the book of Allāh (ﷻ), the Qur'ān will be a proof against them and not for them. Just as the Messenger of Allāh (ﷺ) said, "And the Qur'ān is a proof for you or against you." [Muslim] Allāh (ﷻ) struck an example for those that do not act upon the books that were revealed to them, like the Torah (in relation to the Jews), so He (ﷻ) said:

﴿ مَثَلُ الَّذِينَ حُمِّلُوا التَّوْرَاةَ ثُمَّ لَمْ يَحْمِلُوهَا كَمَثَلِ الْحِمَارِ يَحْمِلُ أَسْفَارًا ۚ بِئْسَ مَثَلُ الْقَوْمِ الَّذِينَ كَذَّبُوا بِآيَاتِ اللَّهِ ۚ وَاللَّهُ لَا يَهْدِي الْقَوْمَ الظَّالِمِينَ ﴿٥﴾ ﴾

The example of those who were entrusted with the Torah, then they did not fulfill it (i.e., its obligations), is as the likeness of a donkey who carries

burdens of books. How bad is the example of the people who deny the verses of Allāh? And Allāh does not guide the oppressive people.

[Sūrah al-Jumu'ah: 5]

This verse, even if it was revealed concerning the Jews who knew the Torah and did not act upon it, it applies upon those who know the Qur'ān and don't act upon it. The Messenger (ﷺ) sought refuge with Allāh (ﷻ) from the knowledge that does not benefit. Thus, he said, "Oh Allāh, verily I seek refuge with You from knowledge that does not benefit." [Muslim] Meaning, knowledge that I do not act upon or convey to others, and it does not improve my character. It also came in another ḥadīth, "Read the Qur'ān and act by it, and do not eat by it." [Authentic, reported by Aḥmed and other than him]

I used to pray in a mosque close to my house, and its imām used to know me. He found that I call to the worship of Allāh, alone, not invoking other than Him. He gave me a book called *That Which is Sufficient in Refuting the Wahhābī*, I think it is by Zaynī Daḥlan, who used to be the Mufti in Makkah before the rule of Saudi Arabia. He said in it, "Verily, there are men who say to something 'be' and it is!" I was astounded by this lie, because this is from the attributes of Allāh, alone, and mankind is incapable of creating a fly. Rather, they are even incapable of retrieve what the fly took from his food. Allāh (ﷻ) struck an example for mankind in which he clarified the weakness of the creation. He (ﷻ) said:

﴿ يَا أَيُّهَا النَّاسُ ضُرِبَ مَثَلٌ فَاسْتَمِعُوا لَهُ ۚ إِنَّ الَّذِينَ تَدْعُونَ مِن دُونِ اللَّهِ لَن يَخْلُقُوا ذُبَابًا وَلَوِ اجْتَمَعُوا لَهُ ۖ وَإِن يَسْلُبْهُمُ الذُّبَابُ شَيْئًا لَّا يَسْتَنقِذُوهُ مِنْهُ ۚ ضَعُفَ الطَّالِبُ وَالْمَطْلُوبُ ﴿٧٣﴾ ﴾

O mankind! A parable has been made, so listen to it. Verily, those on whom you call besides Allāh cannot create a fly, even if they came together to do so. And if the fly snatches away a thing from them, they are not able to take it back from the fly. So weak are the seeker and the sought.

[Sūrah al-Ḥajj: 73]

I took the book to its owner, who had memorized the Qur'ān with me in Dār al-Huffāḍ. I said to him, "This shaykh claims that men say to a thing 'be' and it is. Is this correct?" He told me, "Yes, the Messenger of Allāh (ﷺ) said, 'Be Tha'labah', so it turned out to be Tha'labah!" I asked him, "Did Tha'labah not exist, and he (ﷺ) brought him into existence from nothing? Or was he absent, and the Prophet (ﷺ) was waiting for him, and he was late. And when the Messenger of Allāh (ﷺ) saw an indistinct shape from afar, he became optimistic and said, 'Be Tha'labah.' This was as if he was saying, 'I ask Allāh that the person who is coming be Tha'labah, so the army can move and not run late.' Allāh (ﷻ) answered his supplication, and the person who was coming was Tha'labah." The man went silent, and he knew the falsehood of the speech of the shaykh who authored the book. He still has the book to this day.

A Journey with Jamā'at at-Tablīgh

Jamā'at at-Tablīgh is very active in the Arab and Islāmic countries, and even in foreign countries such as France and other than it.

This group is distinguished by their humility in their travels, sincerity in their propagation, as well as organization in their travelling, eating, and going out for said propagation. Their places of work are the mosques that they come to, and they go to cafés and other than them to call the people there to the mosque to establish the prayer. One of them gives a short speech to the people in the mosque, and this is a good action.

The group has a general leader, and he is Shaykh In'ām al-Ḥasan. He resides in Pakistan. They have a general gathering, and usually it is in Pakistan. In every country, they have a leader whose opinion they take in consultation.

They have a book called *Tablīgh Nisāb* in the Urdu language. It is also known as *Faḍā'il al-'A'amāl.* It has been translated into Arabic, and the scholars have found points of criticism; from the angle of creed, the Sufi ideologies, and other than it. The books that they rely on the most are:

- *Riyāḍ aṣ-Ṣāliḥīn.* It is a good book, especially the copy that has been examined and clarifies the authentic aḥadīth from the inauthentic. It is very important amongst the people of knowledge.
- *The Lives of the Ṣaḥābah.* It is a good book. However, there are weak and fabricated aḥadīth in it. It needs to be investigated, and its narrations checked, as will be clarified soon, if Allāh (ﷻ) wills.

(**Translator's note:** Shaykh Muqbil al-Wādi'ī (رحمه الله) said about *The Lives of the Ṣaḥābah,* "*The Lives of the Ṣaḥābah* has in it aḥadīth that are authentic, aḥadīth that are inauthentic, and aḥadīth that are fabricated, as well as stories that are falsehood. So, it should not be relied upon." [From the audio "Sunni Answers to Tanzanian Questions"])

They have six qualities that they cling to, and they teach them to the members of their group. The discussion of them will come later, and these six are as follows:

1. Actualizing the statement "Lā ilāha Illa Allāh, Muḥammad ar-Rasool Allāh"
2. Establishing the prayer with tranquility and humility
3. Knowledge with dhikr
4. Generosity toward the Muslims

5. Making the intention sincerely for Allāh (ﷻ)
6. Calling to Allāh (ﷻ)

Going Out with Jamā'at at-Tablīgh

I was affected at first by their calling, and I went out with them to a number of lands.

I went with them to the city of Aleppo in which I live. We went to the different mosques, especially on Friday. We went out in a group to a neighborhood in Aleppo called Carlac, which has a large mosque in it. We entered the mosque before the Friday prayer. I went out with my cousin, per the advice of the leader, to the market. We entered a large café where people were playing chess, backgammon, and cards that have images of a child—a girl and a large man. Our assignment was limited to calling the people to attend the prayer. We invited them and they all came, except for a few who promised that they would finish the game and then come to the mosque.

When we finished our roaming in the markets, we went to the mosque. The leader was waiting for us. When we arrived, he gave me the book *Riyāḍ aṣ-Ṣāliḥīn* and requested that I read "From the Etiquettes of the Mosque." I read in it the statement of the Messenger (ﷺ), "Whoever has eaten garlic or onion, then let him stay away from our mosque and let him sit in his house."

[Agreed upon by al-Bukhārī and Muslim] I explained the ḥadīth to those present in the mosque and clarified to them that the smell of smoke (i.e., from cigarettes or other than them) is more severe than the smell of garlic and onion. It is upon the Muslim to stay away from it because it harms his body, harms his neighbor, destroys his wealth, and there is no benefit in smoking. Suddenly, the leader started looking at the book I was reading—and it was *Riyāḍ aṣ-Ṣāliḥīn*—as if he were saying to me, "This speech about smoking isn't in the book, so don't say it!" This is an error. Smoking is widespread amongst the Muslims, even amongst those of them who pray. So, it is necessary that it be warned against, especially during the warning against eating garlic and onion at the time of entering the mosque.

I noticed some weak aḥadīth with Jamā'at at-Tablīgh, so I mentioned that to them. They said to me, "Come with us to the general leader in Jordan and speak to him about it."

I went with the Jamā'at to the city of Ḥamāh. We were knocking on doors. The owner of the house would come out, and the leader would invite him to come to the mosque to gather with them and listen to the lesson and the lecture. I entered upon their leader in their mosque, so he said to those present, "We prostrated to Allāh, so Allāh made the world prostrate to us!!"

This is a tremendous error. Prostration is an act of worship and is not permissible to be done for other than Allāh. Allāh (ﷻ) said:

﴿ فَاسْجُدُوا لِلَّهِ وَاعْبُدُوا ﴿٦٢﴾ ﴾

So prostrate to Allāh and worship Him.

[Sūrah an-Najm: 62]

I also heard a man argue with the leader, saying, "Why do you all separate the religion from politics and say, 'There are no politics in the religion,' despite the fact that the religion has politics in it?" The leader went silent and did not answer, as is the norm with them. I saw a youth smoking at the door of the mosque, and he had a beautiful beard. I advised him to leave off smoking, and I gave him a kūfī as a gift. He put it on his head and threw the cigarette on the ground. The leader found out about this and called for me. He chastised me for it and said, "Let him smoke in the room next to the mosque until he leaves it by himself!" I said, "This is an enormous error to leave him smoking, even if it was in the room that is beside the mosque. The Messenger (ﷺ) said, "Whoever from amongst you sees an evil, then let him change it with his hand, and if he is not able to, then with his tongue, and if he is not able to, then with his heart, and that is the weakest of faith." [Muslim]

We went by the market of Ḥamāh. One of those who were accompanying us said, "I don't want to go by this market because my father will see me and get angry. I left him in the store by himself, and I left my wife by herself in the house, and she is about to give birth." I told him, "This is not permissible in the religion. Go to your father and apologize to him or write him a letter. Go to your wife and ask how she is, because she may be sick or in need of someone who will take care of her and her children. The Messenger of Allāh (ﷺ) said, "It is sufficient as a sin upon a person to not take care of those who rely upon him." [Ḥasan, reported by Aḥmed and other than him]

Then, we went to Damascus and entered Kafar Sousah mosque. A youth had given a reminder after the prayer and mentioned in it a ḥadīth where he said in it, "The worldly life is an abode for those who have no abode." After he finished his speech, I asked him, "Is that an authentic ḥadīth?" He said to me, "I heard it from Jamā'at at-Tablīgh." I told him, "That isn't sufficient." He turned to a man who was a scholar beside him and asked about the ḥadīth. He said to him, "That is not a ḥadīth." Then, I advised him gently to search for the authentic aḥadīth and stay away from the inauthentic and fabricated ones. When their leader saw me, he came to me and told me, "Don't teach him. Allāh will teach him!" Keeping in mind that he gives them classes in fiqh and other than it.

Years passed, and I came to Makkah. I saw the man going to Al-Masjid al-Ḥarām before the Friday prayer. I caught up to him, greeted him, and said, "Are you 'Abū Shākir?" He said to me, "Yes." I said, "You were the one who was in Damascus and said to me, 'Don't teach this youth. Allāh will teach him.'?" He replied, "Yes." I said, "How can you say that while the Messenger of Allāh (ﷺ) said, 'Knowledge is only (gained) by learning.'?" [Ḥasan, refer to Ṣaḥīḥ al-Jāmi'] He told me, "I erred." I advised him to not reject knowledge and advice, with full knowledge that he is a teacher in Ṭā'if, and he had to have been a student before he became a teacher.

I went on a journey with them and there were three of us. We entered a room where the youth were playing cards that they call shiddah, which have images, numbers, and amounts. I spoke with the youths gently and said to them, "This is impermissible and a waste of your time, and it pulls one toward gambling and brings about enmity between its players." They were convinced and began to tear the cards that they used to play with. They gave me some so I could participate in tearing them. Thus, I tore up some of the cards, sharing with them, and earning the reward. Then, they went with us to the prayer in the mosque.

When their leader found out about it, he called me over and criticized me for tearing the cards they had been playing with. I told him "They requested that I participate with them in tearing the cards, so I did so. They were the ones who began tearing the cards before me." However, he did not accept that!

I said to myself, "These people command with good and do not forbid evil, while the Messenger (ﷺ) said, "Whoever from amongst you sees an evil, then let him change it with his hand, and if he is not able to, then with his tongue, and if he is not able to, then with his heart, and that is the weakest of faith." [Muslim]

Then, I went with them to Jordan. They have a large mosque in Amman where they gather. We arrived at the mosque and prayed there, then one of the heads gave a lecture in which he mentioned things that were strange. He said, speaking to those present:

"Oh beloved brothers! Do not eat a lot, so as to not defecate a lot. For Imām Ghazālī went on Ḥajj for a month, and he didn't defecate!" One of those sitting said to him, "Where did you get this story?" He denied it because it is not possible for a person to survive for a month without defecating. Then, the man got up and left the gathering and the mosque.

Then, he said in his lecture, while he was reading from the book *The Lives of the Ṣaḥābah*, "When the Messenger (ﷺ) returned from Ṭā'if, he met with a servant named 'Addās. The Messenger (ﷺ) asked him where he was from. He said he was from Nineveh, so he (ﷺ) said to him, "You are from the land of Yūnūs (عليه السلام). He is my brother in prophethood." So, 'Addās prostrated to the Messenger (ﷺ).

I found this speech strange: How can the Messenger (ﷺ) be pleased with 'Addās prostrating to him while it is not permissible to prostrate to anyone but Allāh (ﷻ)?"

This story is inauthentic. That which is correct is that 'Addās fell to the feet of the Messenger (ﷺ) to kiss them, and this kissing differs entirely from prostration. The book *The Lives of the Ṣaḥābah* needs to be investigated so the authentic, weak, and fabricated aḥadīth can be known. I advised the brother Muḥammad 'Alī Dawlah and requested that he investigate the book because he is the one who printed and spread it. He said to me, "The book is all in virtues, and there are no legislative rulings in it." This is not correct. I brought the ḥadīth to him that the author of *The Lives of the Ṣaḥābah* had brought. It is, "My companions are like stars, so whichever of them you follow, you will be guided by them." I told him the scholars of ḥadīth said about this narration that it is fabricated. The brother Muḥammad 'Alī Dawlah went silent. Then I turned to the Shaykh Nayef al-Abbāsi (rḍ) in Damascus, and I said to him, "I read in the book *The Lives of the Ṣaḥābah*—which you investigated and commented on—that which follows, 'When the Messenger (ṣ) returned from Ṭā'if, and he had called them to Islām, and they refused his call and harmed him, he sat, saying "Oh Allāh, I complain to you of my weakness in my strength, and the small amount of my planning, and my lowliness to the people. Who do you leave me to? To an enemy that will be angry at me, or a relative that You will give control of my affair? If you are not angry at me, I do not care ..."' to the end of the supplication. [Shaykh al-Albānī declared it to be weak.] How can the Messenger (ṣ) say scolding his Lord, 'Who do you leave me to?'?!' Meanwhile, Allāh (ﷻ) says to him:

$$\text{﴿ مَا وَدَّعَكَ رَبُّكَ وَمَا قَلَىٰ ﴾}$$

Your Lord has neither forsaken you, nor hates you.

[Sūrah aḍ-Ḍuḥa: 3]

Shaykh Nayef al-Abbāsi said to me, "By Allāh, your speech is correct. The Messenger of Allāh did not say this speech, but I only investigated the book from a historical and linguistic perspective. This book needs the likes of Ash-Shaykh Nāṣir ad-Dīn al-Albānī to derive its aḥadīth." I told him, "Verily, Shaykh Nāṣir (may Allāh preserve him) declared the ḥadīth to be weak, and said, 'There is something objectionable in the text of the ḥadīth.' Perhaps he's referring to the statement, 'Who do you leave me to?' which opposes the Qur'ān and reality."

I attended a meeting of theirs in which their leader, Sa'īd al-Aḥmad, gave a speech. He said:

"The Messenger (ﷺ) passed by a building, so he said to his companions, 'Who's is this?' They said, 'It's so and so's building.' When the owner of the building passed by the Messenger (ﷺ) said, 'As-Salāmu 'Alaykum' to him, but he did not return the salām. The Ṣaḥābah informed him of the reason, the companion went and destroyed the building, so the Prophet (ﷺ) would return the salām to him."

I said, "This ḥadīth is inauthentic because the Messenger (ﷺ) said, "What good righteous wealth for a righteous man." [Authentic, reported by Aḥmed.]

THE CONDITIONS OF THE JAMĀ'AT

1 – Actualization of the Statement "Lā Ilāha Illa Allāh, Muḥammad ar-Rasool Allāh"

Verily, actualization means understanding and application. So, has this group understood the meaning of this good statement, which is the first pillar from the pillars of Islām that came in the ḥadīth of Jibrīl that Muslim reported? And have they called to the application of it and acting by it?

The reality is that they do not know its true meaning, and it is: "There is no deity worthy of worship except for Allāh, and Muḥammad (ﷺ) is the conveyer of the religion of Allāh that He is pleased with." The evidence of this definition is the statement of Allāh (ﷻ):

﴿ ذَٰلِكَ بِأَنَّ اللَّهَ هُوَ الْحَقُّ وَأَنَّ مَا يَدْعُونَ مِن دُونِهِ هُوَ الْبَاطِلُ ﴿٦٢﴾ ﴾

That is because Allāh is the Truth (The only true deity worthy of worship), and what they invoke besides Him is falsehood.

[Sūrah al-Ḥajj: 62]

If they knew its meaning, they would have called to it before anything else, because it calls to the singling out of Allāh (ﷻ) in worship and supplicating to Him, alone, without other than Him. This is due to the statement of the Messenger of Allāh (ﷺ), "Supplication, it is worship." [Reported by at-Tirmidhī, and he said it is ḥasan ṣaḥīḥ.]

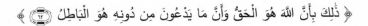

So, just as the prayer is an act of worship done for Allāh (ﷻ) and it is not permissible to be done for a messenger or a saint; likewise, supplication is an act of worship, and it is not permissible to supplicate to a messenger or to saints.

I have not heard Jamā'at at-Tablīgh calling to the understanding of this statement and acting by it. The one who supplicates to other than Allāh (ﷻ) has fallen into polytheism that nullifies all deeds, due to the statement of Allāh (ﷻ):

﴿ وَلَا تَدْعُ مِن دُونِ اللَّهِ مَا لَا يَنفَعُكَ وَلَا يَضُرُّكَ ۖ فَإِن فَعَلْتَ فَإِنَّكَ إِذًا مِّنَ الظَّالِمِينَ ﴿١٠٦﴾ ﴾

And do not call on others beside Allāh who do not benefit you nor harm you, for if you were to do so, you would surely be from the wrongdoers.

[Sūrah Yūnūs: 106]

The meaning of wrongdoers here is polytheists.

2 – Establishing the Prayer with Tranquility and Humility

Establishing the prayer means knowing its conditions, obligations, pillars, and what is connected to it from rulings, such as the prostration of forgetfulness for instance. This is in accordance with what came in the ḥadīth, "Pray as you have seen me pray." [al-Bukhārī]

Has Jamā'at at-Tablīgh taught these matters to their group? Have they clarified to their group that tranquility in the prayer—meaning focusing on recitation, the tasbīḥ, limiting unnecessary movement in the prayer, and other than that—is from the important actions?

3 – Knowledge with Dhikr

This condition, like the rest of the conditions, has not been actualized by Jamā'at at-Tablīgh. I have previously mentioned that I advised one of the youths who gave a speech and mentioned in it a fabricated ḥadīth. Their leader said to me, "Leave him. Do not teach him. Allāh will teach him!" This is despite the fact that the Messenger (ﷺ) says, "Knowledge is only (attained) by learning." [Ḥasan, refer to Ṣaḥīḥ al-Jāmi']

A group of them visited me in Jordan, and I clarified the creed of monotheism to them. From it is the belief that Allāh (ﷻ) is above the heavens, just as Allāh informed of Himself in His statement:

﴿أَأَمِنتُم مَّن فِي السَّمَاءِ أَن يَخْسِفَ بِكُمُ الْأَرْضَ ﴿١٦﴾﴾

Do you feel secure that He who is above the heavens will not cause the earth to sink with you?

[Sūrah al-Mulk: 16]

Ibn 'Abbās said "He is Allāh, the Most High."

I also mentioned to them the ḥadīth of the slave girl, in which the Messenger (ﷺ) asked her, "Where is Allāh?" She said, "In the heavens." Then he said, "Who am I?" She said, "You are the Messenger of Allāh." So, he said to her owner, "Free her, for verily she is a believer." [Muslim]

Those present were astonished by this information. They sought some short books of knowledge from me, although it is known that many of them do not want to read books of knowledge. I gave two of them some treatises as gifts to take them with them and read with their assembly. However, they did not take them. Meanwhile, it is from the guidance of the Prophet (ﷺ) that he used to accept gifts. The Messenger (ﷺ) said, "Give one another gifts and you all will love one another." [Ḥasan, refer to Ṣaḥīḥ al-Jāmi']

4 – Generosity Toward the Muslims

The reality is that they are generous to their guests, especially at the time of food. They speak of generosity towards the scholars. If only they took their advice and accepted their guidance! I went out with them to several places, and not once did they allow me to speak. Rather, they allow one from their group, even if he was ignorant, to speak to the people. This harms more than it benefits, so they come with fabricated aḥadīth, as was mentioned previously. They also come with an inauthentic ḥadīth regarding the time of eating. They say, "Speak at the time of eating, even if it is about the price of your weapons." I did not find it in the books of ḥadīth.

5 – Making the Intention Sincerely for Allāh (ﷻ)

It is an important condition, and some of them may actualize this. They would go with the intention of calling to the religion and spend from their wealth. The place of sincerity is the heart, and none knows it except for Allāh (ﷻ). Their members speak about their calling a lot, especially the leaders. They say that they did such and such, and they were such and such in number, and many people answered their call. I ask Allāh (ﷻ) that they are sincere in their actions. However, it is necessary that sincerity is with knowledge. That way it can benefit them, and the 'Ummah can also benefit. Al-Bukhārī mentioned (رحمه الله) in his book, "Chapter: Knowledge is before statements and actions." He used the statement of Allāh (ﷻ) as evidence:

﴿ فَاعْلَمْ أَنَّهُ لَا إِلَٰهَ إِلَّا اللَّهُ ﴿١٩﴾ ﴾

So know, that there is no deity worthy of worship but Allāh.

[Sūrah Muḥammad: 19]

I have previously stated that Jamā'at at-Tablīgh, may Allāh (ﷻ) guide them, do not concern themselves with knowledge.

6 – Calling to Allāh (ﷻ)

This is a good beginning point. It is obligatory upon every Muslim to give attention to it. It is upon everyone, according to their capability; but calling to Allāh has an important condition that Allāh (ﷻ) clarified in His statement:

﴿ قُلْ هَٰذِهِ سَبِيلِي أَدْعُو إِلَى اللَّهِ ۚ عَلَىٰ بَصِيرَةٍ أَنَا وَمَنِ اتَّبَعَنِي ۖ وَسُبْحَانَ
اللَّهِ وَمَا أَنَا مِنَ الْمُشْرِكِينَ ﴿١٠٨﴾ ﴾

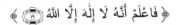

Say, this is my way; I invite unto Allāh upon clear knowledge, I and those who follow me. And Glorified is Allāh; and I am not from the polytheists.

[Sūrah Yūsūf: 108]

Allāh (ﷻ) tells His Messenger (ﷺ) to inform the jinn and mankind that this is His path, method, way, and practice. It is calling to testifying that there is no deity worthy of worship but Allāh, alone, without any partners, calling to Allāh with that upon clarity and certainty, along with legislative and intellectual proof.

Glorified is Allāh, meaning I glorify Allāh (ﷻ), exalt Him, venerate Him, and sanctify Him from there being a partner with Him, or rival, counterpart, equal, child, parent, wife, secretary, or advisor. He is Blessed, Holy, and free from all of that, and high above it. [Refer to Tafsīr ibn Kathīr, vol. 2, pg. 4]

In Summary

Verily, these are their conditions, even if they are not harmonious. However, what this group lacks is the application of these conditions in practice, especially knowledge and actualizing the statement of tawḥīd and calling to it first. The example of this the Messenger of Allāh (ﷺ), who remained in Makkah 13 years calling the people to it and bearing harm in the path of it. He stayed patient until Allāh (ﷻ) made him victorious. The Arabs knew the meaning of tawḥīd in the statement "Lā ilāha illa Allāh." Because of this, they did not accept it. This is because it calls the to the worship of Allāh (ﷻ) and invoking him, alone, and leaving off supplicating other than him, even if they be from the saints and righteous. Allāh (ﷻ) said about the polytheists:

﴿ إِنَّهُمْ كَانُوا إِذَا قِيلَ لَهُمْ لَا إِلَٰهَ إِلَّا اللَّهُ يَسْتَكْبِرُونَ ﴿٣٥﴾ وَيَقُولُونَ أَئِنَّا لَتَارِكُو آلِهَتِنَا لِشَاعِرٍ مَّجْنُونٍ ﴿٣٦﴾ بَلْ جَاءَ بِالْحَقِّ وَصَدَّقَ الْمُرْسَلِينَ ﴿٣٧﴾ ﴾

Verily, when it was said to them, "There is no deity worthy of worship but Allāh," they would become arrogant and say, "Are we going to abandon our gods for a mad poet?" Rather, he has come with the truth, and the messengers were truthful.

[Sūrah aṣ-Ṣaffāt: 35-37]

The Religion is Sincerity

The Messenger of Allāh (ﷺ) said, "The religion is sincerity." We said, "To who, oh Messenger of Allāh?" He (ﷺ) said, "To Allāh, his Book, His Messenger, the leaders of the Muslims, and the general people from amongst them." [Muslim]

Acting upon the statement of this Noble Messenger (ﷺ), I direct my advice to all of the Islāmic groups to abide by what came in the Qur'ān and the authentic ḥadīth, in accordance with the understanding of the pious predecessors (may Allāh be pleased with them) like the companions of the Prophet (ﷺ), the generation that followed them, the imāms of Islāmic jurisprudence, and those who traverse upon their path.

THE COLLECTIVE OF SUFIS

My advice to the Sufis is that they single out Allāh (ﷻ) in their supplication and seeking help acting upon His statement:

﴿ إِيَّاكَ نَعْبُدُ وَإِيَّاكَ نَسْتَعِينُ ۝٥ ﴾

You, alone, we worship, and You, alone, we ask for help.

[Sūrah al-Fātiḥah: 5]

Also, there is the statement of the Messenger of Allāh (ﷺ) "Supplication, it is worship." [Reported by at-Tirmidhī, and he said it is ḥasan ṣaḥīḥ.]

It is upon them to believe that Allāh (ﷻ) is above the heavens, due to the statement of Allāh (ﷻ):

﴿ ءَأَمِنتُم مَّن فِي السَّمَاءِ أَن يَخْسِفَ بِكُمُ الْأَرْضَ ۝١٦ ﴾

Do you feel secure that He who is above the heaven will not cause the earth to sink with you?

[Sūrah al-Mulk: 16]

Ibn 'Abbās said, "He is Allāh.' [Ibn al-Jawzī mentioned it in his tafsīr.]

The Messenger of Allāh (ﷺ) said, "Do you not trust me, and I am the trustee of He who is above the heavens?" [Agreed upon by al-Bukhārī and Muslim]

It is upon them to abide in their dhikr by that which was reported in the Book and the Sunnah, as well as the actions of the companions.

It is upon them that they do not give precedence to the statement of their mashaykh over the statement of Allāh and His Messenger (ﷺ), acting upon the statement of Allāh (ﷻ):

﴿ ا أَيُّهَا الَّذِينَ آمَنُوا لَا تُقَدِّمُوا بَيْنَ يَدَيِ اللَّهِ وَرَسُولِهِ ۝١ ﴾

O you who believe! Do not put yourselves forward before Allāh and His Messenger.

[Sūrah al-Ḥujurāt: 1]

This means, do not put a statement or action before the statement of Allāh (ﷻ) and His Messenger (ﷺ). [Ibn Kathīr mentioned it in his tafsīr.]

It is upon them to worship Allāh (ﷻ), and to supplicate to Him fearing His Fire and hoping for His Paradise, acting upon His (ﷻ) statement:

﴿وَادْعُوهُ خَوْفًا وَطَمَعًا ۝٥٦﴾

And invoke Him with fear and hope.

[Sūrah al-'A'rāf: 56]

The Messenger of Allāh (ﷺ) said, "Ask Allāh for the Paradise, and seek refuge with Him from the Fire." [Reported by 'Abū Dāwūd with an authentic chain of narration]

It is upon the Sufis to believe that the first of the creation from mankind was Ādam (عليه السلام) and that Muḥammad (ﷺ) is from the progeny of Ādam; and all of mankind are from his descendants, and Allāh (ﷻ) created them from dust. Allāh (ﷻ) said:

﴿هُوَ الَّذِي خَلَقَكُم مِّن تُرَابٍ ثُمَّ مِن نُّطْفَةٍ ۝٦٧﴾

He is the One who created you all from dust, then from a drop of sperm.

[Sūrah Ghāfir: 67]

There is not any evidence that Allāh (ﷻ) created Muḥammad (ﷺ) from His Light, and that which is known is that he was born to two parents.

JAMĀ'AT AD-DAWAH WA AT-TABLĪGH

My advice to them is that they abide in their calling by what came in the Book and the authentic sunnah, and to learn the Qur'ān, tafsīr, and ḥadīth. This is so their calling can be founded upon knowledge, due to the statement of Allāh (ﷻ):

﴿ قُلْ هَٰذِهِۦ سَبِيلِىٓ أَدْعُوٓا۟ إِلَى ٱللَّهِ ۚ عَلَىٰ بَصِيرَةٍ ﴿١٠٨﴾ ﴾

Say, "This is my way, I call to Allāh upon clear knowledge.

[Sūrah Yūsūf: 108]

Also, there is the statement of the Messenger (ﷺ), "Knowledge is only attained by learning." [Ḥasan, refer to Ṣaḥīḥ al-Jāmi']

It is upon them as well to aid by the authentic aḥadīth, and stay away from the weak and fabricated aḥadīth, so as to not enter under the statement of the Messenger (ﷺ), "It is sufficient for a man to be a liar that he narrates everything that he hears." [Muslim]

It is upon Jamā'at at-Tablīgh to not separate commanding with good from forbidding evil, because Allāh (ﷻ) joined them in many verses, such as the statement of Allāh (ﷻ):

﴿ وَلْتَكُن مِّنكُمْ أُمَّةٌ يَدْعُونَ إِلَى ٱلْخَيْرِ وَيَأْمُرُونَ بِٱلْمَعْرُوفِ وَيَنْهَوْنَ عَنِ ٱلْمُنكَرِ ۚ وَأُو۟لَٰٓئِكَ هُمُ ٱلْمُفْلِحُونَ ﴿١٠٤﴾ ﴾

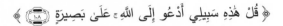

Let there be from you a group of people who call to good, and enjoin the good and forbid the evil, and it is they who are successful.

[Sūrah Ali 'Imrān: 104]

The Messenger of Allāh (ﷺ) gave it great attention and commanded the Muslims to change evil. He (ﷺ) said, "Whoever from amongst you sees an evil, then let him change it with his hand, and if he is not able to, then with his tongue, and if he is not able to, then with his heart, and that is the weakest of faith." [Muslim]

It is upon them to give great concern to calling to tawḥīd, and giving it precedence over other than it, acting upon the statement of the Messenger of Allāh (ﷺ), "Let the first thing that you call them to be the testimony that none has the right to be worshipped but Allāh." [Agreed upon by al-Bukhārī and Muslim] Another narration states, "To single out Allāh (in worship)." [al-Bukhārī] Singling out of Allāh (ﷻ) means singling Him out in worship, especially in supplication, due to his (ﷺ) statement, "Supplication, it is worship." [Reported by at-Tirmidhī, and he said it is ḥasan ṣaḥīḥ.]

The Muslim Brotherhood

My advice to them is that they teach the members of their group tawḥīd with its different types: the oneness of Lordship, the oneness of the right to be worshipped, and oneness of His Names and Attributes. This is because it is extremely important, and the happiness of the individual and the groups depend upon it instead of delving into politics and alleged current events. This does not mean that one should ignore the condition of the countries and people, but it should be done without excessiveness, or carelessness.

I advise them to distance themselves from the ideologies of the Sufis, which oppose the creed of Islām. For we have seen many of them mention the false beliefs of the Sufis in their books.

For example, their leader in Egypt, 'Umar at-Tilmisānī has a book called *The Martyr of the Mihrab*, which contains dangerous beliefs of the Sufis, along with the teaching of music.

In his book *In the Shade of the Qur'ān*, Sayyid Quṭb mentioned the unity of existence, which is a belief of the Sufis. He mentioned it in the beginning of the explanation of Sūrah al-Ḥadīd. He also mentioned other than that from false interpretations. I spoke to his brother, Muḥammad Quṭb and requested that he comment on the errors related to creed being that he oversees the publication of *Ash-Shurūq*. He refused and said, "My brother is responsible for that." The shaykh ‘Abdul Lateef Badr, the director of *Awareness Magazine* in Makkah, encouraged me to revise it.

Sa‘īd Ḥawwā mentioned in his book *Our Spiritual Upbringing* beliefs of the Sufis, and they were mentioned at the beginning of the book.

Muḥammad Ḥāmid from Syria gave me a book named *Refutations of Falsehood* as a gift. It has good points, such as the impermissibility of smoking and other than it, except that he mentioned in it, "Verily, there are 'abdāl, 'aqṭāb, and 'aghwāth." The Sufis claim that there are seven 'abdāl, and they protect seven different regions! (**Translator's note:** This was also stated by Ibn ‘Arabī in *Al-Fatūḥāt al-Makkīyyah*, 2/376, As for 'aghwāth, the quṭb is called ghawth when a person is seeking refuge with him! It is a term for the one who Allāh is looking at in every era. He has given him the greatest talisman from Him. And He and his helpers, who are hidden and apparent, flow in the universe as the soul flows in the body ... and He causes the spirit of life to flow in the highest and lowest of the creation!" [Refer to pg. 75 of *At-Ta‘rīfāt* by Al-Jurjānī]) However, the ghawth is not called a ghawth except when refuge is being sought with him!!!"

Seeking refuge with 'aghwāth and 'aqṭāb is from the shirk that nullifies all good deeds, and it is from the false ideology of the Sufis that Islām rejects. I have asked his son, ‘Abdur Raḥman, to comment on the speech of his father, but he refused to do so.

I advise them to not hate the Salafīs, who call to tawḥīd, combat innovation, and call to ruling by the Book and the Sunnah. This is because they are their brothers in Islām. Allāh (ﷻ) says:

﴿ إِنَّمَا الْمُؤْمِنُونَ إِخْوَةٌ ﴿١٠﴾ ﴾

The believers are not but brothers.

[Sūrah al-Ḥujurāt: 10]

The Messenger of Allāh (ﷺ) said, "Not one of you believe until he loves for his brother what he loves for himself." [Agreed upon by al-Bukhārī and Muslim]

THE SALAFĪS

My advice to them is to continue in their call to tawḥīd, ruling by what Allāh (ﷻ) revealed, and other than that from the important matters.

I advise them to be gentle in their calling, and use gentleness in their speech, no matter who your opponent is. This is in accordance with the statement of Allāh (ﷻ):

﴿ ادْعُ إِلَىٰ سَبِيلِ رَبِّكَ بِالْحِكْمَةِ وَالْمَوْعِظَةِ الْحَسَنَةِ ۖ وَجَادِلْهُم بِالَّتِي هِيَ أَحْسَنُ ﴿١٢٥﴾ ﴾

Call to the Path of your Lord with wisdom and fair preaching and argue with them with that which is best.

[Sūrah an-Naḥl: 125]

And His statement to Mūsā and Harūn, peace be upon them:

﴿ اذْهَبَا إِلَىٰ فِرْعَوْنَ إِنَّهُ طَغَىٰ ﴿٤٣﴾ فَقُولَا لَهُ قَوْلًا لَّيِّنًا لَّعَلَّهُ يَتَذَكَّرُ أَوْ يَخْشَىٰ ﴿٤٤﴾ ﴾

Go to Fir'aun, verily he has transgressed. And say to him gentle speech, so that he may receive admonition or fear Allāh.

[Sūrah Ṭaha: 43-44]

And the statement of the Messenger of Allāh (ﷺ), "Whoever has been deprived of gentleness has been deprived of all good." [Muslim]

It is upon them to be patient upon what befalls them from harm. For verily, Allāh (ﷻ) is with them in His aid and help. Allāh (ﷻ) said:

﴿ وَاصْبِرْ وَمَا صَبْرُكَ إِلَّا بِاللَّهِ ۚ وَلَا تَحْزَنْ عَلَيْهِمْ وَلَا تَكُ فِي ضَيْقٍ مِّمَّا يَمْكُرُونَ ﴿١٢٧﴾ إِنَّ اللَّهَ مَعَ الَّذِينَ اتَّقَوا وَّالَّذِينَ هُم مُّحْسِنُونَ ﴿١٢٨﴾ ﴾

And be patient, for your patience is not but from Allāh. And do not be sad over them, and do not

distress over what they plot. Verily, Allāh is with those who believe and those who do good

[Sūrah an-Naḥl: 127-128]

And the statement of the Prophet (ﷺ), "The believer who mixes with the people and is patient upon their harm is better than the believer who does not mix with the people and is not patient upon their harm." [Authentic, reported by Aḥmed and other than him]

I advise the Salafīs not to look at the statement of those who oppose them, those who say that the Salafīs are few in number, because Allāh (ﷻ) said:

﴿ وَقَلِيلٌ مِّنْ عِبَادِيَ الشَّكُورُ ﴿١٣﴾ ﴾

And few from My slaves are thankful.

[Sūrah Sabā': 13]

And the statement of the Messenger of Allāh (ﷺ), "Glad tidings to the strangers." It was said, "Who are they, Oh Messenger of Allāh?" He said, "A small number of people who are righteous amongst many people who are evil, those who disobey them are more than those who obey them." [Authentic, reported by Aḥmed and Ibn al-Mubārak]

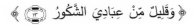

Hizb at-Tahrīr

My advice to them is to implement the teachings of Islām upon themselves before they seek for others to apply them. Two youths from them visited me in Syria 20 years ago. Their faces were shaved, and the smell of cigarette smoke was on them. They sought to have a discussion with me so I could join them. I said to them, "You all shave your faces and smoke, and they are both impermissible in the Sharī'ah. Then you make shaking the hands of women permissible for yourselves, while the Messenger of Allāh (ﷺ) said, "For one of you to have an iron needle driven into his head is better for him than to touch a woman that is not permissible for him." [Authentic, reported by at-Tabarānī]

They said to me, "It was reported in Ṣaḥīḥ al-Bukhārī that the Messenger (ﷺ) shook the hands of the women when they pledged allegiance to him!" So, I said to them, "Tomorrow you will come with the ḥadīth." They left and did not return. Thus, I knew they were liars, and that al-Bukhārī never mentioned that. He only mentioned the women pledging allegiance to the Prophet (ﷺ) without shaking hands.

That which is strange is that some of the Muslim Brotherhood make shaking the hands of women permissible, like Muḥammad al-Ghazālī, and Yūsūf al-Qarḍāwī, with whom I had a debate. He used the ḥadīth of the girl that used to take the hand of the Messenger of Allāh (ﷺ) to answer the call of nature. [Reported by al-Bukhārī]

I said, "The usage of this ḥadīth as an evidence is incorrect, knowing that the girl didn't touch him when she took his hand. Rather, she only took the sleeve of his qamīṣ that was on his hand. This is because ʿĀʾishah (﷡) said, "No, by Allāh, his hand never touched the hand of a woman when pledging allegiance. They did not pledge allegiance to him except with his statement, 'I give you allegiance upon that.'" [al-Bukhārī]

The Messenger of Allāh (ﷺ) said, "Verily, I do not shake hands with the women." [Reported by at-Tirmidhī, and he said it is ḥasan ṣaḥīḥ.]

I heard a sermon from a shaykh who is a member of Hizb at-Tahrīr in Jordan. He is severe against the rulers who rule by other than what Allāh (ﷻ) has revealed. When I came to his house, the father of his wife complained to me about him, and said, "Verily, the shaykh hit his wife in her eye, and it got infected!" I said to the shaykh, "You seek from the rulers to apply the Sharīʿah, while you haven't applied the Sharīʿah in your house! Did you hit your wife in her eye?" He replied, "Yes, but it was a light strike with a cup of tea!"

I said to him, "Apply Islām upon yourself first, then seek its application from others. The Messenger (ﷺ) was asked about the right of one of our wives upon us, so he said, "... to feed them when you eat and get her clothing when you get clothing, and do not strike the face, nor say to her 'May Allāh make you ugly,' nor boycott her except in the house.'" [Authentic, reported by 'Abū Dāwūd, at-Tirmidhī, an-Nasā'ī, and Ibn Majah]

He (ﷺ) also said, "When one of you hits his slave, then let him stay away from the face." [Ḥasan, reported by 'Abū Dāwūd]

JAMĀ'AT AL-JIHAD AND OTHERS

My advice to them is to be gentle in their calling and their striving, especially with the rulers, acting by the statement of Allāh (ﷻ) to Mūsā' when He sent him to Fir'aun the disbeliever:

﴿ اذْهَبْ إِلَىٰ فِرْعَوْنَ إِنَّهُ طَغَىٰ ﴿١٧﴾ فَقُلْ هَل لَّكَ إِلَىٰ أَن تَزَكَّىٰ ﴿١٨﴾ ﴾

Go to Fir'aun. Verily, he has transgressed. And say, "Would you be willing to purify yourself?"

[Sūrah an-Nāzi'āt: 17-18]

Also, the statement the statement of Allāh (ﷻ):

﴿ اذْهَبَا إِلَىٰ فِرْعَوْنَ إِنَّهُ طَغَىٰ ﴿٤٣﴾ فَقُولَا لَهُ قَوْلًا لَّيِّنًا لَّعَلَّهُ يَتَذَكَّرُ أَوْ يَخْشَىٰ ﴿٤٤﴾ ﴾

Go to Fir'aun. Verily, he has transgressed. And say to him gentle speech, so that he may receive admonition or fear Allāh.

[Sūrah Ṭaha: 43-44]

Also, the statement of the Messenger of Allāh (ﷺ), "Whoever has been deprived of gentleness has been deprived of all good." [Muslim]

Advising the leaders of the Muslims and their rulers is by aiding them upon the truth and obeying them in that. This is done by obeying their commands and prohibitions, reminding them with gentleness, and leaving off rebelling against them with the sword when oppression or bad dealings appear from them. [Refer to the statement of Al-Khaṭṭābī in the *Explanation of the Forty Ḥadīth*]

The author of *Al-'Aqīdah aṭ-Ṭaḥāwiyyah*, 'Abū Ja'far aṭ-Ṭaḥāwī, said, "We do not believe in rebelling against our leaders and rulers, even if they were oppressive. And we do not supplicate against them, and do not remove a hand from their obedience. We see the obedience of them as being from the obedience of Allāh (ﷻ) and obligatory as long as they do not command with sin, and we supplicate for them with rectification and forgiveness."

Allāh (ﷻ) said:

﴿ يَا أَيُّهَا الَّذِينَ آمَنُوا أَطِيعُوا اللَّهَ وَأَطِيعُوا الرَّسُولَ وَأُولِي الْأَمْرِ مِنكُمْ ﴿٥٩﴾ ﴾

O you who have believed! Obey Allāh, and obey the Messenger, and those in authority from amongst you.

[Sūrah an-Nisā': 59]

The Messenger of Allāh (ﷺ) said, "Whoever obeys me, then he has surely obeyed Allāh, and whoever disobeys me then he has surely disobeyed Allāh; and whoever obeys the ruler, then he has surely obeyed me, and whoever disobeys the ruler then he has surely disobeyed me." [al-Bukhārī and Muslim]

On the authority of Abi Dharr (ﷺ), he said, "Verily, my close companion (i.e., the Messenger of Allāh [ﷺ]) advised me to listen and obey, even if the ruler was an Abyssinian slave" [Muslim]

The Messenger of Allāh (ﷺ) said, "It is upon the person to listen and obey in that which he loves and hates, unless he is commanded with sin. For if he is commanded with sin, then there is no hearing and no obeying." [Agreed upon by al-Bukhārī and Muslim]

On the authority of Ḥudhayfah ibn al-Yamān (ﷺ), he said, "The people used to ask the Messenger of Allāh (ﷺ) about good, and I would ask him about evil out of fear that it would reach me. I said, 'Oh Messenger of Allāh! Verily, we were in ignorance and evil, so Allāh came to us with this good. Is there any evil after this good?' He said, 'Yes.' So, I said, 'Is there any good after that evil?' He said, 'Yes, and there is smoke in it.' I said, 'And what is its smoke?' He said, 'A people who follow other than my Sunnah and seek guidance from other than my guidance. You will see from them that which you will know to be good and that which is blameworthy.' I said, 'Is there evil after that good?' He said, 'Yes, callers to the gates of Hell. Whoever answers their call is thrown into the Fire.' I said to him, "Oh Messenger of Allāh, describe them to us!' He said, 'Yes, they are a people from our flesh who speak our language.' I said, "Oh Messenger of Allāh, what do you advise with if that reaches me?' He said, 'Cling to the group of the Muslims and their leader.' I said, "And if there isn't a group of Muslims, nor a leader at that time?' He said, 'Then separate yourself from all of those sects, even if you were to bite at the root of a tree until death reaches you, and you are upon that.'" [Agreed upon by al-Bukhārī and Muslim]

The Messenger of Allāh (ﷺ) said, "Whoever sees something that he hates from his leader, then let him be patient. For verily, whoever splits from the Jamā'ah, and dies will die as those who have died in the pre-Islāmic state of ignorance." [Agreed upon by al-Bukhārī and Muslim]

He (ﷺ) said, "The best of your rulers are those who you love and they love you, and they pray for you and you pray for them; and the worst of your rulers are the ones that you hate and they hate you, and you curse them, and they curse you." We said, "Oh Messenger of Allāh! Should we not oppose them with the sword at that time?" He said, "No, as long as they establish the prayer amongst you. Verily, whoever has a leader appointed over him and sees him doing something from disobedience to Allāh, then let him hate what he does from disobedience to Allāh, and not remove a hand from obedience to him." [Muslim]

The Book and the Sunnah indicate the obligation of obedience to the rulers, as long as they do not command with sin. Thus, contemplate the statement of Allāh (ﷻ):

﴿ أَطِيعُوا اللَّهَ وَأَطِيعُوا الرَّسُولَ وَأُولِي الْأَمْرِ مِنكُمْ ﴿٥٩﴾ ﴾

Obey Allāh, and obey the Messenger, and those in authority from amongst you.

[Sūrah an-Nisā': 59]

Contemplate upon how He (ﷻ) said:

﴿ وَأَطِيعُوا الرَّسُولَ ﴾

And obey the Messenger.

He did not say, "... and obey those in authority from amongst you," because those in authority are not singled out in obedience. Rather, they are obeyed in that which is obedience to Allāh (ﷻ) and His Messenger (ﷺ). He repeated the verb with the Messenger (ﷺ) because whoever obeys the Messenger (ﷺ) has surely obeyed Allāh (ﷻ). Verily, the Messenger does not command with other than the obedience of Allāh. Rather, he (ﷺ) is infallible in that. As for the ruler, he might command with other than the obedience of Allāh (ﷻ), so he is not obeyed except in what is in obedience to Allāh and His Messenger (ﷺ).

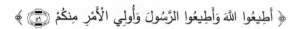

As for obeying them even if they are oppressive; it is because the evils that result from deviating from the obedience of them are many times more than that which occurs from their oppression. Rather, in patience upon their oppression is an expiation of sins and multiplying of rewards. For Allāh (ﷻ) has not placed them over us except because of our corrupt actions, and the recompense is from the nature of the action. Therefore, it is upon us to seek forgiveness, repent, and rectify our actions. Allāh (ﷻ) said:

﴿ وَمَا أَصَابَكُم مِّن مُّصِيبَةٍ فَبِمَا كَسَبَتْ أَيْدِيكُمْ وَيَعْفُو عَن كَثِيرٍ ﴿٣٠﴾ ﴾

And what befalls you from calamities is by what your hands have earned, and He forgives much.

[Sūrah ash-Shūrā: 30]

And He (ﷻ) said:

﴿ وَكَذَٰلِكَ نُوَلِّي بَعْضَ الظَّالِمِينَ بَعْضًا بِمَا كَانُوا يَكْسِبُونَ ﴿١٢٩﴾ ﴾

And like this do we make the wrongdoers supporters to one another because of that which they used to earn.

[Sūrah al-An'ām: 129]

If those being ruled over want to get rid of the oppression of the oppressive leader, then let them leave off oppression. [Refer to the Explanation of Al-'Aqīdah aṭ-Ṭaḥāwiyyah, pgs. 380 to 381]

Striving with the Muslim rulers is by giving advice to them and their aids, due to the statement of the Messenger of Allāh (ﷺ),

"The religion is sincerity." We said, "To who, Oh Messenger of Allāh?" He said, "To Allāh, His Book, His Messenger, the leaders of the Muslims, and the general people." [Muslim]

Also, his (ﷺ) statement, "The best jihad is a truthful word in the presence of an oppressive ruler." [The ḥadīth is ḥasan, and was reported by 'Abū Dāwūd and at-Tirmidhī]

And to clarify, the method of being freed from the oppression of the rulers who are from our flesh and speak our language is for the Muslims to repent to their Lord (ﷻ), rectify their creed, and cultivate themselves and their families upon the correct Islām, actualizing the statement of Allāh (ﷻ):

﴿ إِنَّ اللَّهَ لَا يُغَيِّرُ مَا بِقَوْمٍ حَتَّىٰ يُغَيِّرُوا مَا بِأَنفُسِهِمْ ﴿١١﴾ ﴾

Verily, Allāh does not change the condition of a people until they change that which is with themselves.

[Sūrah ar-Ra'd: 11]

One of the present-day callers alluded to that with his statement, "Establish an Islāmic country in your hearts, and it will be established for you in your land." Likewise, it is necessary that the foundation be rectified to build the building upon it, and that foundation is the community. Allāh (ﷻ) said:

﴿ وَعَدَ اللَّهُ الَّذِينَ آمَنُوا مِنكُمْ وَعَمِلُوا الصَّالِحَاتِ لَيَسْتَخْلِفَنَّهُمْ فِي الْأَرْضِ كَمَا اسْتَخْلَفَ الَّذِينَ مِن قَبْلِهِمْ وَلَيُمَكِّنَنَّ لَهُمْ دِينَهُمُ الَّذِي ارْتَضَىٰ لَهُمْ وَلَيُبَدِّلَنَّهُم مِّن بَعْدِ خَوْفِهِمْ أَمْنًا ۚ يَعْبُدُونَنِي لَا يُشْرِكُونَ بِي شَيْئًا ۚ وَمَن كَفَرَ بَعْدَ ذَٰلِكَ فَأُولَٰئِكَ هُمُ الْفَاسِقُونَ ﴿٥٥﴾ ﴾

Allāh has promised those who have believed from amongst you and do good deeds that He will certainly grant the succession in the earth just as He granted it to those before them, and He will establish for them their religion that He is pleased with for them, and He will change their fear to security, provided they worship me and do not associate with me anything in worship. And whoever disbelieves after that, then they are from the rebellious.

[Sūrah an-Nūr: 55]

[Summarized from the book Commentary on the Explanation of aṭ-Ṭaḥāwiyyah by Shaykh al-Albānī]

My Advice to All of the Groups

I have reached the extent of old age, and my age is now close to 70 years. I want good for all of the groups, acting upon the statement of the Messenger (ﷺ), "The religion is advice." [Muslim]

Therefore, I present the following advices:

1 – To cling to the Qur'ān, and the prophetic sunnah, acting upon the statement of Allāh (ﷻ):

﴿ وَاعْتَصِمُوا بِحَبْلِ اللَّهِ جَمِيعًا وَلَا تَفَرَّقُوا ﴿١٠٣﴾ ﴾

And hold fast to the rope of Allāh together and do not be divided.

[Sūrah 'Ali 'Imrān: 103]

Also, the statement of the Messenger of Allāh (ﷺ), "I have left two things amongst you. You will not go astray as long as you cling to them, the book of Allāh and the sunnah of His Messenger." [Reported by Mālik and graded as authentic by al-Albānī in Ṣaḥīḥ al-Jāmi']

2 – When the groups differ, it is upon them to return to the Qur'ān, ḥadīth, and actions of the Ṣaḥābah, acting upon the statement of Allāh (ﷻ):

﴿ فَإِن تَنَازَعْتُمْ فِي شَيْءٍ فَرُدُّوهُ إِلَى اللَّهِ وَالرَّسُولِ إِن كُنتُمْ تُؤْمِنُونَ بِاللَّهِ
وَالْيَوْمِ الْآخِرِ ۚ ذَٰلِكَ خَيْرٌ وَأَحْسَنُ تَأْوِيلًا ﴿٥٩﴾ ﴾

So, if you differ in anything, then return it to Allāh and the Messenger, if you believe in Allāh and the Last Day. That is better and has the best result.

[Sūrah an-Nisā': 59]

Also, the statement of the Messenger (ﷺ), "It is upon you to cling to my sunnah and the sunnah of the rightly guided caliphs." [Authentic, reported by Aḥmed]

3 – Give great concern to the creed of tawḥīd that the Qur'ān focused on, and the Messenger (ﷺ) began his call to it and commanded his companions to begin with it.

4 – I have had close dealings with the Islāmic groups and have seen that the Salafī dawah clings to the Book and the Sunnah according to the understanding of the pious predecessors, the Messenger (ﷺ), his companions, and the generation who followed them. The Messenger of Allāh (ﷺ) alluded to this group with his statement, "Verily, those before you from the people of the Book split into 72 sects. And verily, this nation will split into 73 sects, 72 in the Fire, and one of them in the Paradise, and it is the Jamā'ah." [Reported by Aḥmed, and Ibn Hajr declared it to be ḥasan] In another narration, "All of them are in the Fire except one, what I and my companions are upon." [Reported by at-Tirmidhī and al-Albānī declared it to be ḥasan]

The Messenger of Allāh (ﷺ) informed us that the Jews and the Christians split much, and the Muslims will split more than them, and that these sects will be subjected to entering the Fire due to their deviation and distance from the Book of their Lord and the Sunnah of their Prophet (ﷺ). That one sect will be saved from the Fire and enter the Paradise, and it is the group that clings to the book, the sunnah, and the actions of the Ṣaḥābah.

The Salafī call is distinguished by its calling to tawḥīd and combatting shirk, knowing the authentic aḥadīth and warning from weak and fabricated aḥadīth, and knowing the legislative rulings with their evidences; and this is very important for every Muslim.

I advise my Muslim brothers to cling to the Salafī dawah, because it is the Saved Sect, and the Victorious Group that the Messenger of Allāh (ﷺ) said concerning it, "There is a group from my nation who will not cease to remain victorious upon the truth. They will not be harmed by those who forsake them, until the Command of Allāh comes." [Muslim]

Oh Allāh, make us from the Saved Sect, and the Victorious Group.

In Summary

It is upon the Islāmic groups to distance themselves from hated partisanship that leads to splitting, and to aid one another amongst themselves in that which benefits the Muslims and gives them good and benefit, due to the statement of Allāh (ﷻ):

﴿ وَتَعَاوَنُوا عَلَى الْبِرِّ وَالتَّقْوَىٰ ۖ وَلَا تَعَاوَنُوا عَلَى الْإِثْمِ وَالْعُدْوَانِ ۚ ﴾

And cooperate in righteousness and piety, and do not aid one another in sin and transgression.

[Sūrah al-Mā'idah: 2]

Also, the statement of the Messenger (ﷺ), "Be slaves of Allāh and brothers. The Muslim is the brother of the Muslim. He does not oppress him, nor forsake him, nor belittle him. Piety is here, and he pointed to his chest. It is sufficient as evil for a person to belittle his Muslim brother. All of the Muslims to other Muslims are sacred, his blood, his wealth, and his honor." [Muslim]

It is upon the Islāmic groups to not be envious of one another, nor hate one another, due to his (ﷺ) statement, "Do not envy one another, and do not hate one another, and do not turn away from one another." [Muslim]

It is upon every group from the Islāmic groups to accept advice if it agrees with the Qur'ān and the authentic aḥadīth, due to his (ﷺ) statement, "The religion is sincerity." [Muslim] Also, his (ﷺ) statement, "All of the children of Ādam err, and the best of those who err are the repentant." [Ḥasan, reported by Aḥmed and other than him]

I close my statement with the following supplication:

Oh Allāh, rectify that which is between us, and join our hearts, and guide us to the paths of peace. Oh Allāh, make us guided and cause us to guide others. Do not make us astray or cause us to lead others astray. Make us at peace with your allies and at war with your enemies. And may Allāh send His salutations and peace upon Muḥammad (ﷺ) and his relatives and followers.

ADDITIONAL REMARKS

Allāh (ﷻ) has blessed me. I have begun to call to the tawḥīd of Allāh (ﷻ) and published more than 20 books. All of them have been printed a number of times in large amounts, and some of them have been translated into English, French, Indonesian, Urdu, Bengali, Turkish, and other than them. Most of these books were printed with the help of benefactors and given out for free. Some of them are sold in the bookstores that print them from their own money, and I have written on every book the following phrase, "Every Muslim has the right to print and translate this book, and whoever has any observation on the books, then let him please inform the author."

A book from the Emirates reached me, with the title *The Creed of the Imām, the Ḥāfiḍ Ibn Kathīr* by Muḥammad Adil Azīzah. When I read it, I found that he did not cling to the integrity of knowledge, even in the prophetic aḥadīth, whereas he cut out the ḥadīth that Ibn Kathīr mentioned in explanation of the statement of Allāh (ﷻ):

﴿ يَوْمَ يُكْشَفُ عَن سَاقٍ ﴿٤٢﴾ ﴾

The day that the shin will be uncovered

[Sūrah al-Qalam: 42]

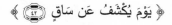

Also, the statement of the Messenger of Allāh (ﷺ), "Our Lord will uncover His shin, so every believing man and woman will prostrate to Him ..." to the end of the ḥadīth that al-Bukhārī and Muslim reported.

He, Muḥammad Adil Azeezah, said in his book, "Muḥammad Jamīl Zeno stumbled in his book *The Methodology of the Saved Sect*, severely on page 16 and other than it." And Allāh (ﷻ) knows that I became happy, and said, "Perhaps I made and error, and will rectify my error." When I looked in my book that was mentioned, I found the following, "Imām Aḥmed said, 'Imām Ash-Shāfi'ī said, "Al-Khatīb al-Baghdadī ..."'" So, I called the author and told him, "What is the stumbling that you mentioned in my book?" He said to me, "I don't have the book with me." So, I said to him, "Why did you remove the ḥadīth that explains the verse from *Tafsīr Ibn Kathīr*?" He said to me, "The ḥadīth is from that which is unclear!!" I said to him, "And why did you remove the statement of Ibn Kathīr in his tafsīr:

﴿ وَهُوَ اللَّهُ فِي السَّمَاوَاتِ ﴿٣﴾ ﴾

And He is Allāh (to be worshipped) in the heavens.

[Sūrah al-An'ām: 3]

Where he chose the statement of the mufassir aṭ-Ṭabari, to affirm that Allāh (ﷻ) is above the heavens?" He said to me, "Wait until I look," and he did not admit to his mistake. I refuted this author in a book called *Clarification and Warning from the Book "The Creed of the Imām", the Hāfiḍ Ibn Kathīr.*

I read in a book titled *In the Prophetic School*, by the brother Aḥmad Muḥammad Jamāl, that he said in it, "I was surprised by the brother Muḥammad Jamīl Zeno when he wrote in *The Nadwah* newspaper on the 26th of Rabī' ath-Thānī 1411 AH, and denounced the wording of the salutations that are sent upon the Messenger (ﷺ) that many people are used to saying. And it is their statement, "Oh Allāh, send your blessings upon Muḥammad (ﷺ), the medicine of the hearts, and their remedy and the good health of the body and their cure, and the light of the eyes and their radiance." He also said, "Verily, the once who cures and gives good health to the bodies, hearts, and eyes is Allāh, alone; and the Messenger doesn't have dominion over benefit for himself nor other than them ..." to the end of his statement. I would like the brother Muḥammad Zeno to know that this wording has two correct understandings:

1 – The medicine of the hearts, good health of the bodies, and the light of the eyes is an attribute, or a fruit of the salutations sent upon the Messenger (ﷺ). We have known from the previous aḥadīth the virtue of the salutations upon the Messenger (ﷺ) and its blessings, and that it comes from Allāh (ﷻ). The Salutation of Allāh upon His slaves is mercy, blessings, good health, and a cure.

2 – The medicine of the hearts, and the good health of the bodies, and the light of the eyes is an attribute for the Messenger (ﷺ)

himself. This has nothing blameworthy in it, nor any strangeness. The Messenger (ﷺ), his essence as the Noble Qur'ān described it, is a mercy. It is the statement of Allāh (ﷻ):

﴿ وَمَا أَرْسَلْنَاكَ إِلَّا رَحْمَةً لِّلْعَالَمِينَ ﴿١٠٧﴾ ﴾

And We have not sent you except as a mercy to the creation.

[Sūrah al-'Anbiyā: 107]

He is also light and radiance, as the Qur'ān described him in His (ﷻ) statement:

﴿ يَا أَيُّهَا النَّبِيُّ إِنَّا أَرْسَلْنَاكَ شَاهِدًا وَمُبَشِّرًا وَنَذِيرًا ﴿٤٥﴾ وَدَاعِيًا إِلَى اللَّهِ بِإِذْنِهِ وَسِرَاجًا مُّنِيرًا ﴿٤٦﴾ ﴾

Oh Prophet, verily We have sent you as a witness, a bearer of glad tidings, and a warner. And a caller to Allāh, by His permission, and an illuminating lamp.

[Sūrah al-Aḥzāb: 45-46]

In multiple narrations, the Messenger (ﷺ) describes himself as a mercy that has been given as a gift to mankind to remove it from darkness to light, and cure the hearts and the visions and the bodies from the literal and figurative diseases together. He (ﷺ) said, "I am only a mercy that has been given as a gift." [Ibn 'Asākir]

"Verily, I am a mercy that Allāh has sent." [at-Tabarānī]

"I have not been sent as one who slanders. I have only been sent as a mercy." [Muslim]

I say the previously mentioned wording that the author claims the people are accustomed to using is not permissible, because sending the salutations upon the Prophet (ﷺ) is an act of worship. The general rule with worship is that it is not done until the evidence comes for it, and there is no evidence for that wording, especially because it opposes all of the narrations that were reported on the Messenger (ﷺ) and his companions, and the pious predecessors. Also, there is excessiveness and glorifying in it that Allāh (ﷻ) and the Messenger (ﷺ) are not pleased with. Therefore, is it permissible for the Muslim to leave off the wording that the Messenger (ﷺ) used with his companions, and take wording from the statements of the people who oppose the legislated wording?

The author removed something important from my speech, and it is my usage of the statement of Allāh (ﷻ):

﴿ قُل لَّآ أَمْلِكُ لِنَفْسِي نَفْعًا وَلَا ضَرًّا إِلَّا مَا شَاءَ اللَّهُ ﴿١٨٨﴾ ﴾

Say, "I do not possess for myself benefit nor harm except that which Allāh wills."

[Sūrah al-'A'rāf: 188]

Also, the statement of the Messenger of Allāh (ﷺ), "Do not raise me above my level as the Christians raised (Jesus) the son of Maryam, for I am only a slave. So, say, 'the slave of Allāh and His Messenger.'" [al-Bukhārī]

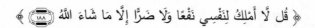

As for the statement of the writer, "... and the salutations of Allāh upon his slaves are mercy, blessings, good health, and cure." Ibn Kathīr said, "The salutations from Allāh, the Most High, upon His servant are His praise amongst the angels." Also, it was said, "The salutations from Allāh the Mighty and Majestic are mercy. [Refer to *Tafsīr ibn Kathīr*, vol. 3, pg. 495]

This is the correct explanation that reveals the falsehood of the explanation of the author Aḥmed Muḥammad Jamāl, which has no evidence for it.

As for his using as evidence the statement of Allāh (ﷻ):

﴿ وَمَا أَرْسَلْنَاكَ إِلَّا رَحْمَةً لِّلْعَالَمِينَ ﴿١٠٧﴾ ﴾

And We have not sent you except as a mercy for the creation.

[Sūrah al-'Anbiyā': 107]

I will quote for the reader that which the 'Allāmah Muḥammad al-Amīn ash-Shinqītī said in explanation of the verse, "... and the statement of Allāh (ﷻ) mentioned in this verse, "He has not sent him except as a mercy to the creation," indicates that he came with mercy for the creation in what this Great Qur'ān contains." This meaning has come clarified in different places in the Book of Allāh, such as His (ﷻ) statement:

﴿ أَوَلَمْ يَكْفِهِمْ أَنَّا أَنزَلْنَا عَلَيْكَ الْكِتَابَ يُتْلَىٰ عَلَيْهِمْ ۚ إِنَّ فِي ذَٰلِكَ لَرَحْمَةً
وَذِكْرَىٰ لِقَوْمٍ يُؤْمِنُونَ ﴿٥١﴾ ﴾

Has it not sufficed them that We sent down to you the book which is recited to them? Verily, in that is a mercy and reminder for a people who believe.

[Sūrah al-'Ankabūt: 51)

Also, His (ﷻ) statement:

﴿ وَمَا كُنتَ تَرْجُو أَن يُلْقَىٰ إِلَيْكَ الْكِتَابُ إِلَّا رَحْمَةً مِّن رَّبِّكَ ﴿٨٦﴾ ﴾

And you did not expect that the book would be sent down to you, but it is a mercy from your Lord.

[Sūrah al-Qaṣaṣ: 86]

On the authority of 'Abū Hurayrah (ﷺ), he said, "It was said, 'Oh Messenger of Allāh! Supplicate against the polytheists!' So he said, 'Verily, I have not been sent as one who curses. I have only been sent as a mercy.'" [Muslim]

[Refer to Adhwā al Bayān by ash-Shinqītī, vol. 4, pg. 694]

As for aṭ-Ṭabari, he said that which can be summarized as, "Allāh sent Muḥammad (ﷺ) as a mercy for the entirety of the world, the believers from them and the disbelievers from them. As for the believers from them, Allāh guided them by way of the Prophet (ﷺ) and by them believing in him and what he brought from Allāh (ﷻ), He entered them into Paradise. As for the disbelievers from them, he removed the immediate calamity that used to come down upon the nations that disbelieved in their messengers before them."

As for the statement of the author, "And he (meaning the Messenger [ﷺ]) is light and radiance, as the Qur'ān described him in the statement of Allāh (ﷻ):

﴿ يَا أَيُّهَا النَّبِيُّ إِنَّا أَرْسَلْنَاكَ شَاهِدًا وَمُبَشِّرًا وَنَذِيرًا ﴿٤٥﴾ وَدَاعِيًا إِلَى اللَّهِ بِإِذْنِهِ وَسِرَاجًا مُّنِيرًا ﴿٤٦﴾ ﴾

Oh Prophet, verily We have sent you as a witness, a bearer of glad tidings, and a warner. And a caller to Allāh by His permission and an illuminating lamp

[Sūrah al-'Aḥzāb: 45-46]

I will quote for the reader what the scholars of tafsīr say:

Ibn Kathīr said in his tafsīr:

"Oh Prophet! Verily, We have sent you as a witness upon your nation, a giver of glad tidings of the Paradise and a warner from the Fire, and a caller to the testimony that there is no deity worthy of worship but Allāh by His permission, and an illuminating lamp with the Qur'ān." And the statement of Allāh (ﷻ):

﴿ شَاهِدًا ﴾

A witness

Meaning: a witness for Allāh with His oneness, and that there is no deity worthy of worship other than Him. Also, it means being a witness of the people and their actions on the Day of Judgement:

﴿ فَكَيْفَ إِذَا جِئْنَا مِن كُلِّ أُمَّةٍ بِشَهِيدٍ وَجِئْنَا بِكَ عَلَىٰ هَٰؤُلَاءِ شَهِيدًا ﴿٤١﴾ ﴾

And We have brought you as a witness against these people.

[Sūrah an-Nisā': 41]

Also, His (ﷺ) statement:

﴿ وَمُبَشِّرًا وَنَذِيرًا ﴾

And a bearer of glad tidings and a warner

Meaning: a bearer of glad tidings of a tremendous reward for the believers, and a warner of a destructive punishment for the disbelievers.

And His (ﷺ) statement:

﴿ وَدَاعِيًا إِلَى اللهِ بِإِذْنِهِ ﴾

And a caller to Allāh by His permission

Meaning: a caller for the creation to the worship of their Lord on the authority of His command.

And His (ﷺ) statement:

﴿ وَسِرَاجًا مُنِيرًا ﴾

And an illuminating lamp

Meaning: and your affair is clear in that which you have come with from the truth, like the sun in its rising and radiance. None deny it except for an obstinate person. [Refer to *Tafsīr ibn Kathīr*, vol. 3, pg. 497]

Ibn al-Jawzī said in his tafsīr, *The Provisions of the Path*:

وَسِرَاجًا مُنِيرًا

And an illuminating lamp

Meaning: you are a lamp for whoever follows you, like a radiating lamp in the dark by which guidance is sought. [Vol. 6, pg. 400]

Aṭ-Ṭabari said in his tafsīr:

وَسِرَاجًا مُنِيرًا

And an illuminating lamp

Meaning: an illumination for His creation with the light that you have come to them with from Allāh (ﷻ). And it is only intended by that, that he guides with it whoever follows him from his nation. [Quoting from aṭ-Ṭabari in summary]

The author said in his book *In the School of Prophethood*:

"... and in multiple narrations, the Messenger (ﷺ) describes himself as being "a mercy given as a gift" to mankind to remove it from darkness to light and cure their hearts and visions from the literal and figurative diseases, altogether. The Prophet (ﷺ) says, "I am only a mercy that was given as a gift." [Authentic; refer to Ṣaḥīḥ al-Jāmi'.] Also, "Verily, I am a mercy. Allāh has sent me." [The ḥadīth before it supports this ḥadīth] Also, "I have not been sent as a curser, and I have only been sent as a mercy." [Muslim]

I say, Verily, the speech of the author Aḥmed Muḥammad Jamāl has some observations made upon it.

The author didn't mention any evidence for his speech except that which he reported from the ḥadīth, "I am only a mercy that has been given as a gift." The Allāmah's explanation of mercy in the verse has been mentioned previously, that the Messenger (ﷺ) came with mercy for the creation in that which is found in this Great Qur'ān.

As for the statement of the author, "... to remove mankind from darkness to light," if only the author returned to the tafsīr of Ibn Kathīr, where he said about it:

﴿ لِتُخْرِجَ النَّاسَ مِنَ الظُّلُمَاتِ إِلَى النُّورِ ﴿١﴾ ﴾

To remove the people from the darknesses to the light

[Sūrah 'Ibrāhīm: 1]

Meaning: We have only sent you, Oh Muḥammad (ﷺ), with this Book to remove the people from what they are in from misguidance and sin to the guidance and the correct way. Allāh (ﷻ) said:

﴿ هُوَ الَّذِي يُنَزِّلُ عَلَىٰ عَبْدِهِ آيَاتٍ بَيِّنَاتٍ لِّيُخْرِجَكُم مِّنَ الظُّلُمَاتِ إِلَى النُّورِ ﴿٩﴾ ﴾

He is the One who sends down upon His slave clear verses to remove you all from darkness into light.

[Sūrah al-Ḥadīd: 9]

The verses are clear that He removes the people from the darkness to the light with the Qur'ān, which has been sent down upon him.

As for the statement of the author, "... and cures their hearts and visions from the physical and figurative diseases together," he intends by the Prophet (ﷺ)!

He did not come with clear evidence for that, with full knowledge that the One who cures diseases is Allāh alone. Allāh (ﷻ) said upon the tongue of 'Ibrāhīm (عليه السلام):

﴿ وَإِذَا مَرِضْتُ فَهُوَ يَشْفِينِ ﴿٨٠﴾ ﴾

And when I become sick, it is He who cures me.

[Sūrah ash-Shu'arā': 80]

He gave emphasis to this using the pronoun that is separated, to emphasize that the Curer is Allāh alone. The Messenger of Allāh (ﷺ) said, "Oh Allāh, Lord of mankind, remove this disease and cure, You are the Curer, there is no cure except for Your cure,

cure with a cure that does not leave any sickness behind." [al-Bukhārī]

And the story of the child and the blind man that came in the ḥadīth is a proof that the Curer is Allāh, alone. For it came in it that the blind man came to the child with many gifts and said to him, "I will give them all to you if you cure me." He said, "Verily, I don't cure anyone. Only Allāh cures. So, if you believe in Allāh, I will supplicate to Allāh for you, and he will cure you." Thus, he believed in Allāh, and he supplicated for him, so Allāh cured him. [Reported by Muslim, ḥadīth 3005]

So, the previously mentioned verse and aḥadīth are proofs that the one who cures is Allāh (ﷻ) alone, and the author Aḥmad Muḥammad Jamāl did not mention one example in which the Messenger (ﷺ) states that he cures, as he claimed. This is a matter that is very dangerous, due his statement (ﷺ), "Whoever says upon me that which I didn't say, then let him take his seat in the Fire." [Ḥasan, reported by Aḥmad]

I asked the Noble Shaykh ibn Bāz, the Mufti of Saudi, about the speech of Aḥmad Muḥammad Jamāl. He said, "Verily, he is a mushrik."

In Summary

The speech of the author, Aḥmad Muḥammad Jamāl has no evidence, and in it is excessiveness and exaggeration in praise, which the Messenger of Allāh (ﷺ) prohibited, saying:

"Be warned of excessiveness in the religion, for those before you were only destroyed by excessiveness in the religion." [Authentic, reported by Aḥmed]

"Do not raise me above my level as the Christians raised (Jesus) the Son of Maryam above his level. For I am only a slave, so say the slave of Allāh and His Messenger." [al-Bukhārī]

Especially when the author claimed that the Messenger (ﷺ) states that he cures the hearts and the visions from the physical and figurative diseases! The word "cures" is a present tense verb that indicates the present and future tense, and this is not possible ever. This curing has not happened in the present time, nor will it happen in the future.

What I have mentioned from the alerts on the book *In the School of Prophethood* is from the angle of advice is generally for the Muslims, and specifically for the readers of the mentioned book.

I ask Allāh (ﷻ) to benefit the Muslims by it and make it solely for the sake of Allāh (ﷻ).

An Important Notice

I say, the Messenger (ﷺ) has performed many miracles. However, they were in his lifetime, and these are examples of them.

On the authority of 'Abdullāh ibn Mas'ūd (ﷺ) that he said, "We were traveling with the Messenger of Allāh (ﷺ), and we ran low on water. The Messenger (ﷺ) said, "Bring to me the remaining water." The Ṣaḥābah came with a vessel that had a little water in it. The Messenger (ﷺ) entered his hand into the vessel and said, "Come to the blessed pure water, and the blessing is from Allāh." Ibn Mas'ūd said, "I saw the water spring from between the fingers of the Messenger (ﷺ), and we used to hear the tasbīḥ of the food as it was being eaten." [al-Bukhārī]

The Messenger (ﷺ) drew the attention of his companions to the fact that the blessed water that sprang from between his fingers was only blessed by Allāh, alone, Who created this miracle. This is diligence from the Messenger (ﷺ) upon guiding his nation to tawḥīd, and due to this he said to them, "... and the blessing is from Allāh."

'Alī (ﷺ) came to the Messenger of Allāh (ﷺ) about his eyes. The Messenger (ﷺ) blew spittle into his eyes and supplicated for him. He was cured as if he did not have any ailment in it. [al-Bukhārī]

I say, these miracles were in his lifetime, and the Messenger (ﷺ) supplicated for 'Alī after he blew spittle into his eyes. So, he was cured because the supplication of the Prophet (ﷺ) is answered. As for after his (ﷺ) death, seeking supplication from him has stopped, and the miracles have stopped due to his statement (ﷺ), "When a person dies, his actions are cut off except for three: continuous charity, or knowledge which is benefitted from, or a righteous child who supplicates for him." [Muslim]

'Abū Tālib, the uncle of the Messenger (ﷺ), who used to defend him, when death came to him, the Messenger (ﷺ) called him to the true faith, but he rejected it and died a polytheist. Thus, the verse was revealed about him:

﴿ إِنَّكَ لَا تَهْدِي مَنْ أَحْبَبْتَ وَلَٰكِنَّ اللَّهَ يَهْدِي مَن يَشَاءُ ﴿٥٦﴾ ﴾

Verily, you do not guide those whom you love,
but Allāh guides who He wills.

[Sūrat al-Qaṣaṣ: 56]

[al-Bukhārī]